CHAUCER
The Earlier Poetry

Other Works by Derek Traversi

An Approach to Shakespeare (1938; revised, 1956 and 1968)
Shakespeare: The Last Phase (1954)
Shakespeare: From Richard II *to* Henry V (1957)
Shakespeare: The Early Comedies (1960)
Shakespeare: The Roman Plays (1963)
T. S. Eliot: The Longer Poems (1976)
The Literary Imagination: Studies in Dante, Chaucer, and Shakespeare (1982)
The Canterbury Tales: A Reading (1983)

CHAUCER
The Earlier Poetry

A Study in Poetic Development

Derek Traversi

Newark: University of Delaware Press
London and Toronto: Associated University Presses

© 1987 by Associated University Presses, Inc.

Associated University Presses
440 Forsgate Drive
Cranbury, NJ 08512

Associated University Presses
25 Sicilian Avenue
London WC1A 2QH, England

Associated University Presses
2133 Royal Windsor Drive
Unit 1
Mississauga, Ontario
Canada L5J 1K5

The paper used in this publication meets the requirements
of the American National Standard for Permanence of Paper
for Printed Library Materials Z39.48-1984.

Library of Congress Cataloging-in-Publication Data

Traversi, Derek Antona, 1912–
  Chaucer : the earlier poetry.

  Bibliography: p.
  Includes index.
  Contents: Language and poetics in Chaucer's early
poetry—The Book of the Duchess—The House of fame—
[etc.]
  1. Chaucer, Geoffrey, d. 1400—Criticism and
interpretation. I. Title.
PR1924.T67 1987   821'.1   85-41047
ISBN 0-87413-306-8 (alk. paper)

Printed in the United States of America

Contents

Author's Note		7
1	Language and Poetics in Chaucer's Early Poetry	11
2	*The Book of the Duchess*	33
3	*The House of Fame*	54
4	*The Parliament of Fowls*	78
5	*Troilus and Criseyde*	102
6	Postscript	145
Notes		147
Bibliography		151
Index		153

Author's Note

The studies that make up this book are intended to trace the development of Chaucer's understanding of the potentialities and limitations of his art that led finally to The Canterbury Tales. The first three works considered—The Book of the Duchess, The House of Fame, and The Parliament of Fowls—are recognized by scholars as representing important stages in this process, but are perhaps still less familiar than they deserve to be to the intelligent general reader of poetry. The penultimate chapter, on Troilus and Criseyde, sets out to show how the process traced in the earlier part of the book led to the first unquestioned masterpiece of "modern" English literature and to the definitive incorporation of that literature into the wider European tradition.

One other point calls for comment. In writing of medieval literature the critic finds it necessary to discuss religious and philosophical notions that are still capable of inspiring varying degrees of assent or dissent from modern readers. In view of this it becomes necessary to stress that the critic, as such, is not concerned with whatever degree of "truth" the ideas that emerge from his subject may contain. Indeed, it is at least doubtful whether the authors of the works in question were primarily concerned, as writers and at the moment of writing, with the question of truth as reflected in their creations. The test of the truth of any doctrine or idea advanced in their work probably presented itself to them, as it must certainly do to the critic interpreting the work, in terms of its power to give life and coherence to the chosen material. A poem, or any other work of art, is what it says and says what it is; any attempt to impose exclusive "meaning" or a constricting "moral" upon what is offered in the process of artistic creation as a response to the rich, unpredictable, and disturbing material that life offers to the imagination in its moments of greatest intensity is likely to prove at best irrelevant and at worst destructive of the essential nature of the undertaking.

CHAUCER
The Earlier Poetry

1
Language and Poetics in Chaucer's Early Poetry

At the end of *Troilus and Criseyde* Chaucer takes leave of his poem—the "litel boke," as he somewhat deprecatingly calls it—with an address that reads as follows:

> . . . litel boke, no makyng thow n'envie,
> But subgit be to alle poesye;
> And kis the steppes, where as thow seest pace
> Virgile, Ovide, Omer, Lucan, and Stace.
>
> (5. 1789–92)*

The address is important inasmuch as it tells us something of what the poet intended, and hoped he had achieved in writing his poem. He is claiming to incorporate his work into the tradition of "high" poetry, asserting that he has been able to do in his native English what his great predecessor Dante was conscious of having achieved in his own "lingua volgare."[1] It is significant that the classical poets mentioned are substantially those whom Dante conceived as living "without hope and with desire"[2] in the gracious but pallid Elysian fields, to which the great pagan poets are confined in the fourth canto of the *Inferno*.

Chaucer is saying, in effect, that it is possible, in spite of the lack of a comparable tradition and the uncertain nature of the language,[3] to create in English a poem that its author can justifiably present as worthy to set by the side of the great works that represent what we can call the

---

*Edition used throughout this study: Geoffrey Chaucer, *Works*, ed. F. N. Robinson, 2d ed. (Boston, 1959).

"classical" tradition. He is also saying, with an air of justified pride, that this is what he has just done, for himself and the language that he is serving, in the first long poem that he has brought to a convincing conclusion.

Indeed, when seen from this point of view, Chaucer's earlier work can be regarded as a series of approximations to this goal. At the moment in which he set out to write—somewhere in the late 1360s—he is likely to have felt that the possibility of achieving a work of this kind was at last open to a writer in English; but he must also have felt the lack in what he inherited from the past of an instrument of expression adequate to the purposes he had in mind, a lack due in no small measure to the hiatus produced as long as three hundred years before by the Norman Conquest in the culture to which he belonged and which only now it seemed possible, naturally and spontaneously, to fill.

Past history, indeed, was still in however diminishing measure, a determining influence in the young Chaucer's present. The great pre-Conquest tradition of Anglo-Saxon writing, the product of a period in which the presence of England in Europe was perhaps as great as it has ever been, had been either destroyed or submerged by that traumatic event of 1066; and the alien Norman-French tradition, which might conceivably have taken its place in the educated mind, had no comparable strength to enable it to serve as a replacement. Only in the days of Chaucer's youth, perhaps, was it possible to think of this separation entirely and naturally as a thing of the past; and even then a poet setting out to write with an ambitious literary purpose in his mind must have been aware, as he compared the work available to him in English with the long and impressive achievement of poetry in Latin, of the slightness of the foundations on which he had to build. Dante too had been aware of the problem and had addressed himself to the solution of its linguistic aspect in the *De Volgari Eloquentia;* but Dante had the advantage of a closer connection with the great Latin authors, and though Vergil appears to him at the opening of his great poem as one who addresses him in a desert and across a long silence,[4] he is a consistently living presence, a firm and lofty voice speaking from the very heart of the conception of the *Commedia*.

For Chaucer the work of the great poets of antiquity, venerable as they were, represented a more remote presence. To an English poet conscious of his Englishness and setting out in the second half of the fourteenth century to write for an aristocratic and sophisticated audience, it must have seemed natural to look initially for the models he required to the most advanced literary culture immediately available: to look, in other words, to the poetry that was being written, and had been written, on the other side of the Channel in France. Chaucer's early work can largely be thought of in terms of an attempt to make the French achievement

Language and Poetics in Chaucer's Early Poetry

live in the distinctive terms of his own language. This implies, for example, the preoccupation, evident in all his early poetry, with the dream convention, which presented itself to him as a way—useful, if finally unsatisfactory—to say things that seemed to be important. More immediately, from the point of view of the present argument, it also accounts for his efforts—which again came to seem unsatisfactory for the ends that finally defined themselves to him—to use the short octosyllabic line as he found it in the French writers most readily available to him for imitation and emulation.

We know from Chaucer's own declaration that he translated at least a part of that immensely influential work in French, *Le Roman de la Rose*,[5] though we cannot be certain how much, if any, of the fragments of a translation we possess are in fact his work.[6] Beyond that, we also know that in writing his own early poetry he turned to the example of the French writers of his own time: Froissart, Deschamps, and—more particularly—Guillaume Machaut, whose work, especially the poem entitled *Le Jugement du Roy de Behaigne*, makes its presence felt in *The Book of the Duchess*.

The virtues, and the limitations, of this kind of writing played an important part in Chaucer's early attempts to find a content and a style suitable for his purposes. They can readily be illustrated by quotation. Here is an example from the early lines of *The Book of the Duchess*:

> So when I saw I might not slepe
> Til now late, this other night,
> Upon my bed I sat upright
> And bad oon reche me a book,
> A romaunce, and he it me tok
> To rede, and drive the night away;
> For me thoughte it beter play
> Than play either at ches or tables.
> And in this bok were written fables
> That clerkes had in olde tyme,
> And other poets, put in rime
> To rede, and for to be in minde,
> While men loved the lawe of kinde.
> This bok ne spak but of such thinges,
> Of quenes lives, and of kinges,
> And many other thinges smale.
> Amonge al this I fond a tale
> That me thoughte a wonder thing.
>
> (44–61)

The virtues do not call for a great deal of elaboration. The rhymes, which become in the long run a little monotonous, are designed to advance the narrative, to make us follow the development of events in accordance with a clear, logical purpose. They can, where necessary, induce us to pause on an important word or idea, underlining it in such a way that it stands out for attention; such is the case where the emphasis falls on "upright," on the uncomfortable interruption of the normal conditions of rest, or—more important—on the notion of the "law of kind," which is destined to play an important part in the poem. Nor are the rhythms, and their relationship to the development of the situation described, merely automatic or unsubtly fitted to the couplets. The sense can carry over, develop across the limits apparently imposed—"I might not slepe / Til now late"—and the effect of the rhyme is normally to carry the logical development a stage further, inducing us to follow it with a sense of easy, uninterrupted narrative progression:

> this other night,
> Upon my bed I sat *upright*,
> And bad oon reche me a book,
> A *romaunce*, and he it me tok
> *To rede*, and drive the night away.

We are consistently induced to lay a certain stress on the words underlined and so to let the sense play easily, but not ineffectively, across the apparent regularity of the containing scheme. The result is a kind of clarity, a limpid straightforwardness in exposition, and the consequent ability to advance an argument unobtrusively and directly. Though, as I shall argue shortly, this is a style that has its limitations, it represents virtues that Chaucer was able in due course to incorporate into his own very individual achievement.

The same kind of writing shows itself to be capable, in certain parts of the translation of *The Romaunt of the Rose* (whether the translation is actually Chaucer's work is, for this purpose, immaterial), of dealing intelligibly with a complex theme covering a variety of philosophical, moral, and allegorical matter. In particular it was capable, in the process of bringing the allegorical theme to life, of producing such a sharply pointed "portrait" as the following, of the personification called "Daunger," or Disdain:

> With that sterte oute anoon Daunger,
> Out of the place where he was hid,
> His malice in his chere was kid:
> Full gret he was and blak of hewe,
> Sturdy and hidous, whoso hym knewe.
> Like sharp urchouns his her was growe;
> His eyes reed sparclyng as the fyr glowe;

His nose frounced, full kirked stood.
He com criand as he were wood,
And seide, "Bialacoil, telle me why
Thou bryngest hider so booldely
Hym that so nygh (is) the roser?"

(3130–41)

We may feel here, as elsewhere, that the original "French" content is modified, rendered alive (for an English reader) by a vivid, visualized quality that conveys itself in an unmistakable "Englishness" of speech. The effect of comparing Daunger's upstanding hair to "sharp urchins," of the red eyes "sparkling" like the glow of fire, of the nose "frounced" and "full kirked" ("crooked"?), of the general impression of madness ("as he were wood")—all these things, taken together, amount to an effect that reminds us of certain "portraits" in *Piers Plowman*.[7] They certainly belong to the same tradition, answering to the same medieval tendency to confer a distinctive life, sharply and immediately realized, upon what began as allegorical abstraction.

In the same way, and at greater length, we may feel the presence of a distinctively "dramatic" content in the later exchange between Love and the allegorical representation of Fals-Semblant, or Hypocrisy. The passage is long, but needs to be quoted in full:

"Soth is, but I am an ypocrite."
"Thou gost and prechest poverte."
"Ye, sir, but richesse hath pouste."
"Thou prechest abstinence also."
"Sir, I wole fillen, so mote I go,
My paunche of good mete and wyn,
As shulde a maister of dyvyn;
For how that I me pover feyne,
Yit alle pore folk I disdeyne.
    I love bettir th' acqueyntaunce,
Ten tymes, of the kyng of Fraunce
Than of a pore man of mylde mod,
Though that his soule be also god.
For whanne I see beggers quakyng,
Naked on myxnes al stynkyng,
For hungre crie, and eke for care,
I entremete not of her fare.
They ben so pore and ful of pyne,
They myght not oonys yeve me dyne,
For they have nothing but her lyf.
What shulde he yeve that likketh his knyf?
It is but foly to entremete,

> To seke in houndes nest fat mete.
> Lete bere hem to the spitel anoon,
> But for me, comfort gete they noon.
> But a riche sik usurer
> Wolde I visite and drawe ner;
> Hym wole I comforte and rehete,
> For I hope of his gold to gete."
>
> (6482–6510)

The didactic purpose that motivates the passage is abundantly clear. What is written is evidently offered for our edification; but the edification will be more effective if it is dramatized as a dialogue and if the types are brought to life, visualized, in order to subject them to ironic exposure. This is basically the technique that Chaucer in his maturity will put to use in such figures as the Wife of Bath, more especially in the self-presentation of her prologue,[8] in the character of Hubert the Friar,[9] and in that masterly combination of the sinister, the grotesque, and the comic which is the Pardoner's self-dramatization.[10] Just as the first part of the *Romaunt*—that ascribed to Guillaume de Lorris—gave Chaucer something of the limpidity of style and essentially civilizing courtliness (and we should not confuse the virtues to which he sometimes gives the general name of *gentillesse* with any merely "snobbish" or aristocratic content), so Jean de Meun's more powerful "dramatic" development of the resources of allegory may have introduced him to some of the virtues that are developed to such splendid effect in the *Canterbury Tales*.

The emergence in Chaucer's early work of this distinctive "dramatic" note is connected with the ability to break up the sense of smooth regularity that the line he has chosen seems to impose by allowing the cadences and inflections, the varied stresses of the speaking voice, to play vividly across them. Chaucer from the first shows himself capable of putting this kind of effect to good use, as this account in *The Book of the Duchess* of the awakening of Morpheus, the god of sleep, by Juno's messenger will show:

> This messager com fleynge faste
> And cried, "O, ho! awake anoon!"
> Hit was for noght; there herde hym non.
> "Awake!" quod he, "whoo ys lyth there?"
> And blew his horn ryght in here eere,
> And cried "Awaketh!" wonder hye.
> This god of slep with hys oon ye
> Cast up, axed, "Who clepeth ther?"
> "Hyt am I," quod this messager,
> "Juno bad thow shuldest goon."
>
> (178–87)

What interests us here is the poet's ability to play across the line in such a way as to emphasize his more important effects and, with this, his ability to visualize and to "dramatize" a scene so as to bring it to life in a personal and individual way, which the verse form, in itself, might have been expected to muffle. In its own slight way this kind of writing already looks forward to the great achievement of the most successful passages in *Troilus and Criseyde*.

The achievement, indeed, has important implications for Chaucer's future poetry. Other examples, rather different in kind but pointing in the same direction, can be found in that strange and perhaps significantly unfinished poem, *The House of Fame*.[11] Typical, for example, from the second book is the learned Eagle explaining the scientific truth of things to the poet, who represents himself (not quite so naively as he seems to want us to believe) as bemused and frightened in the predicament of one unwillingly borne up into the higher regions of the air and—as we might say—of theoretical speculation. It is important to respond to the handling of the octosyllabic line, which has grown considerably in versatility and strength since the writing of *The Book of the Duchess*. The passage opens on a note of closely woven and effective dialogue:

> With that this egle gan to crye,
> "Lat be," quod he, "thy fantasye!
> Wilt thou lere of sterres aught?"
> "Nay, certeynly," quod y, "ryght naught."
> "And why?" "For y am now to old."
> "Elles I wolde the have told,"
> Quod he, "the sterres names, lo,
> And al the hevenes sygnes therto,
> And which they ben." "No fors," quod y.
> "Yis pardee!" quod he; "wostow why?
> For when thou redest poetrie,
> How goddes gonne stellifye
> Bridd, fisshe, best, or him or here,
> As the Raven, or eyther Bere,
> Or Arionis harpe fyn,
> Castor, Pollux, or Delphyn,
> Or Athalantes doughtres sevene,
> How alle these are set in hevene;
> For though thou have hem ofte on honde,
> Yet nostow not wher that they stonde."
>
> (991–1010)

The speeches run, where necessary, across the rhyming scheme, which yet serves to hold them together as a developing interchange. The Eagle presses its "doctrine" insistently upon the poet, dismissing his preoccupations as "fantasye"—the word will be a favorite one in the later works,[12] where it generally indicates man's natural, invincible capacity for self-deception—and offering him insistently true teaching on that most poetic of subjects: the "stars." The uneasy poet disclaims any wish to receive this learning: "'Nay, certeynly,' quod y, 'ryght naught,'" where the rhyme with the preceding "aught" effectively underlines the rejection.

The Eagle is not so easily put off, and the exchange tightens notably as the dialogue proceeds. The next line—"'And why?' 'For y am to old'"—suggests the poet seeking to wriggle pathetically out of the doctrinal grip in which he finds himself. The "learned" bird presses on with its offer in two and a half lines about the "sterres names" and the "hevenes sygnes." Good academic that it is, it is *determined* to communicate its knowledge, and once more the poet is left—again at the end of a line, and with a new rhyme to stress the reaction—to insist ineffectively, "No fors." His teacher, however, is by now fully launched on its lecture. Its reply to the poet's plea—at the opening of a new line that is tied to the preceding one by the rhyme—is a ruthless "Yis, pardee," backed by the even greater insistence of "wostow why?" "Clearly not" is the implication and the Eagle proceeds to accept this gleefully as an invitation to tell. It is the pupil's *business,* as poet and even as reader of poetry, to know about the stars and the goals that correspond to them. There is a world of unobtrusive skepticism in the use of the word *stellify,* again stressed by the rhyme. As poet, Chaucer may be assumed to have these mythological matters—and they are listed at learned length—very much "on honde." They are part of the stock in trade of any self-respecting author; how absurd, then, that this particular poet is unaware even of the position of the constellations about which he writes!

Thus urged to consider his inadequacy, Chaucer allows himself a mild, deliberately ineffective self-defense (1011–24). There is no need—"No fors," again—for him to know for himself what he can easily take over from the work of other and more learned authors. Besides, in the uncomfortable position of eminence in which he so unwillingly finds himself, the brilliance of the stars is such that it overcomes

>   al my syghte
> To loke on hem.

Once again the line is broken at the middle to allow the Eagle to proceed implacably on its didactic path. "That may wel be," it comments dismissively, and proceeds on its course—

>   so forth bar he me
> A while—

carrying its unwilling pupil with it. It, at least, knows where it is going, and so, in the next line, it announces triumphantly the arrival of both—teacher and disciple together—at their destination, the House of Fame.

In the lines that follow, the Eagle describes for the benefit of its pupil the mass of confused sound—"the grete swogh"—that emerges from the House and attempts to assuage the poet's sense of his uncomfortable situation:

> "What?" quod I. "The grete soun,"
> Quod he, "that rumbleth up and doun
> In Fames Hous, full of tydynges,
> Bothe of feir speche and chidynges,
> And of fals and soth compouned.
> Herke wel; hyt is not rouned.
> Herestow not the grete swogh?"
> "Yis, parde!" quod y, "wel ynogh."
> "And what soun is it lyk?" quod hee.
> "Peter! lyk betynge of the see,"
> Quod y, ayen the roches holowe,
> Whan tempest doth the shippes swalowe;
> And lat a man stonde, out of doute,
> A myle thens, and here hyt route;
> Or elles lyk the last humblynge
> After the clappe of a thundringe,
> Whan Joves hath the air ybete.
> But yt doth me for fere swete!"
> "Nay, dred the not therof," quod he;
> "Hyt is nothing will byten the;
> Thou shalt non harm have trewely."
>
> (1025–45)

The lines very noticeably gather a force and momentum, which are broken only by the poet's rueful recognition:

> "Herestow not the grete swogh?"
> "Yis, parde!" quod y, "wel ynogh";

the effect of the timid "Yis" is one that Chaucer will put to good use later in his poetic career.[13] The bird, meanwhile, is determined that its pupil should be brought to knowledge by the traditional method of extracting answers to its questionings; and so it presses remorselessly, pedantically, on: "And what soun is it lyk?" Pressed in this way the pupil is moved, however unwillingly, to introduce a new note of poetry into the exchange, when he compares what he hears to nothing less than the "betyng of the see" and "the clappe of a thundrynge" when Jove is in his angry mood. Moved by his own eloquence, so unexpected and so effective, the poet again confesses his fear, only to have it again brushed aside by his self-appointed mentor. "'Nay, dred the not therof,' quod he"; for, as the bird puts it with the familiar jocularity of a master addressing his bemused disciple, "Hyt is nothing will byten thee."

Enough has been said to show that Chaucer's use of the octosyllabic line is reaching out to effects of some complexity. Behind this passage there lies, of course, the preoccupation with dream which Dante—who is here very much in mind—put to such different use in his poem. There is a passage in the *Purgatorio* in which he, too, is borne by an eagle to the lofty regions of the heavens:[14] and, of course, a great part of the *Paradiso* is devoted to the process by which Beatrice, guiding her protégé upward through the celestial spheres, expounds to him in scholastic discourse the nature of the universe. To note these parallels, however, is to be aware of essential differences. Dante, as befits his poem, is throughout the serious poet confident, even in his moments of human fear, of his mission. Chaucer is already in this early poem, as he will always be, a more gently deprecating and skeptical presence, one inclined to be distrustful of "missions" and of those who, like the Eagle, are only too willing to lay claim to them. It is a fundamental difference of attitude, and one that has produced two very different kinds of great poetry.

In *The House of Fame*, indeed, far more clearly than in his previous work, we can see Chaucer arriving at a fuller understanding of the instrument at his disposal and, with it, a clearer conception of the kind of poetry he wished to write. *The House of Fame* gives us the sense of a poetry bursting out of its initial confinements, unwilling to submit to the constricting framework imposed by the rhyming scheme, the monotonously short line, and indeed by the whole "dream" convention. Being the true poet he was, Chaucer formulated this dissatisfaction by squeezing the maximum of possible effect out of the forms he had chosen, and in the process transformed them; but the dissatisfaction is there and will eventually lead him to look for other, more adequate means of expression. The conventions used in the poem can, when it is so required, attain an impressive degree of expository clarity, as, for example, in the long-drawn-out and admirably handled comparison between the spreading of the voices of Rumour and the effect of throwing a stone into a pool (2. 782–822), an example, incidentally, that ends very typically in the gentle skepticism of the final line—"Take yt in ernest or in game"—which, once again, announces a main theme of the poet's mature work.[15]

At the last, the sense with which this significantly unfinished poem leaves us is one of impressions breaking in from every side with the imperious force of "real life," imposing themselves in a kind of disordered wealth that reflects the "real" as distinct from the merely literary world.

We may feel, as we read the concluding stages, a growing sense of the poet's need to express an essentially new vision of things, for which the old schemes are no longer adequate and which is coming to demand new and more appropriate vehicles of expression. If the poem breaks off abruptly, just at the moment when we have been led to expect a decisive revelation (of what?) from the "man of gret auctorite" (2158), it was perhaps because the solution proposed by authority had come—even when expressed with the genius of Dante—to seem abstract, removed from the ever-changing and renewing reality of life, as the verse of its expression was proving increasingly thin and remote in relation to what the poet felt he *now* needed to say.

The discovery of these new forms of expression was, evidently, closely connected for Chaucer with his turning from the short octosyllabic line to the longer unit used in *The Parliament of Fowls*.[16] To read the opening stanzas of this work is to enter a different poetic world:

> The lyf so short, the craft so longe to lerne,
> Th'assay so hard, so sharp the conquerynge,
> The dredful joye, alwey that slit so yerne:
> Al this mene I by Love, that my felynge
> Astonyeth with his wonderful werkynge
> So sore, iwis, that whan I on hym thynke,
> Nat wot I wel wher that I flete or synke.
>
> For al be that I knowe nat Love in dede,
> Ne wot how that he quiteth folk here hyre,
> Yit happeth me full ofte in bokes reede
> Of his myrakles and his crewel yre.
> There rede I wel he wol be lord and syre;
> I dar not seyn, his strokes been so sore,
> But "God save swich a lord!"—I can na moore.
>
> (1–14)

The passage calls for consideration on a variety of levels, of which the first is that of prosody; but a consideration of prosody in this case will take us—as it always will when it is critically used—into matters that point beyond itself to take us into the heart of Chaucer's poetic purposes.

In the first place we should note the presence, within the stanza form (which was again taken from the French), of two distinct effects, effects that are not conflicting, or destructive of one another, but that combine in a new and distinctive voice. The lines that compose the stanza are, considered from one point of view, what prosodists are agreed in calling *iambic pentameters*. They can evidently be "scanned" so as to make the stresses fall in a way that answers to this form, and to do this is to give them a shape that is clearly relevant to the effect they make. This, however, is by no means the whole story. Beneath this effect, both modifying and strengthening the general purpose, is another kind of rhythmic structure, which we may associate with the long and very distinctively English tradition of the alliterative line as it was used most obviously, in Chaucer's own day, by the author of *Piers Plowman*. Indeed, it could be argued that the concept of scansion, which produced the iambic pentameter, is in some degree the result of adapting schemes appropriate to Latin (and perhaps, though less surely, to French and Italian verse) to a language that relies less on equally stressed syllables than on varied and essentially unequal, changing speech rhythms. It could even be said that Shakespeare's supposedly familiar blank verse pentameter is largely a mechanical abstraction and that the reality of the Shakespearean line, as spoken, corresponds more closely to a four-stress line; so that we have not so much

To be´ | or not´ | to be´ | : that is´ | the question,´

as something like "To be / or not to be /: that / is the question." The line, as scanned in the second instance, is less mechanical, closer to the real and varied modulations of the actual speaking voice.

I have already suggested, in dealing with *The Book of the Duchess* and *The House of Fame*, that it is important to avoid the metronome effect,[17] the mechanical beat, which an insensitive application of the conventional scansion imposes. Even within the limits imposed by the octosyllabic line, Chaucer's verse, which we must think of in some measure as being read by an author making full use of the personal inflections of his speaking voice, is not to be delivered in a kind of mechanical sing-song that bends sense and fluctuating feeling to an abstract pattern. At most, the pattern is a foundation, across which the emotional content may move with a very considerable degree of freedom. When in *The Parliament* we pass to the longer and potentially more varied line, this becomes even more important. In the stanzas I have quoted, the pattern of the pentameter is felt to fall naturally into *two* units, normally with *two* stresses in each, making the total of *four* stresses to which I have referred. The effect is no longer one of five approximately equal "feet" answering to what can easily become a mechanical beat—

∪ ´ | ∪ ´ | ∪ ´ | ∪ ´ | ∪ ´ —

(though the effect survives, and serves in an important way to unite the line), but rather of a four-stress line marked—normally, though not necessarily, at a point round the middle—by a deliberate break, which the rhythm of natural speech imposes. To this break the first part of the line builds up, in a kind of ascent, and from it the second part not less deliberately falls.

To show, in the lines quoted, how this rhythmic structure works within the newly discovered stanza is to see a great poet moving toward a fuller awareness of his artistic purposes. It is significant that the two stanzas are expressly concerned with the poet's craft, and emphasize the difficulty, the unending nature of the struggle with words and forms. The first stanza opens with a familiar aphorism—it is a translation of *Ars longa, vita brevis*[18]—which is then expanded in a way prescribed by the rhetorical conventions through which medieval literature tended to express its high and sententious purposes, its sense of what constituted conscious art. The example of the great writers of the past—the poet's "tradition," so to say—is an essential part of the effect, and Ovid is in fact brought into play in the latter part (11-13) of the second stanza. Chaucer is serving notice that he has a serious literary purpose in view and that the perfection of his medium, the mastery of the terms of his craft, is a necessary and difficult condition of success.

In effect, however, the conventions are not only being used to express this kind of purpose but, almost more important, are adapted in their expression to the subtle and shifting rhythms of an unmistakable speaking voice. In the first two lines the sense of effort, of a difficult and painful conquest, is brought home to us through the use made of the divided line. As the voice rises to the central stress, answering to the logic of the contrast, and then—in the second half-line—falling away from it, we can feel the poet's struggle to achieve the aim he has in mind—that of mastering the craft that is so necessary and so difficult, "so long to learn"—and translating it into poetry. The effect, of course, will be more immediately grasped inasmuch as we are able to think of the lines as spoken, or read, avoiding the mechanical beat of the pentameter and allowing ourselves to hear, and to share in, the strain and difficulty that the poet's aim imposes.

From this it is natural to pass, in the third line, to the emphasis on an aspect of this struggle in which the poet is so painfully engaged: on the "*dreadful* love" that constitutes his central theme. The effect is underlined by the word *alwey*—placed, to gain the full benefit of stress, at the opening of the second half line—with its sense of "ever," "unendingly." This again is reinforced by the contrast of all that is implied in "slit": the process, coextensive with life itself, by which what seems to heve been achieved is continually slipping away "so yerne." The poet's theme at this point is nothing less than the unending, and necessary, death of what is always on the point of seeming success, fixed in the final, but illusory perfection of its hard-won expression in words.

The fourth line brings us, with its stressed clarification—"Al this mene I by Love"—to a new stage in the argument. *Love*, as always in Chaucer, means very much more than we, as readers in the twentieth century, can readily associate with the word. *Love*, in this sense, is the inspiration and the appropriate subject matter of poetry. The poet is one who is called upon to deal with this subject matter, and it is significant that, having opened his poem with a discussion of his craft, he should find it natural to say, without marking a transition in his theme, that what he is speaking about is not poetry or language, but *Love*.

Having shifted the terms of his discourse, Chaucer goes on in the last lines of the first stanza to speak of his own emotional condition, which is that of a man—now no longer primarily a poet, or craftsman—engaged in a struggle with dominating and essentially unmanageable states of feeling. This emerges in the words that follow the reference to love as his real theme:

> Al this mene I by Love, that my felynge
> Astonyeth with his wonderful werkynge
> So sore.

What we have here is the contrast, effectively emphasized by the placing of the words in relation to the line-division, between "feeling," which is personal, even tragic in its implications, and the stress on continual, unending "astonishment." The latter word carries a sense of the sheer dominating *unexpectedness* of the real, the actually lived: the unexpectedness that gives reality to the forms of the poet's craft, making what he writes not a mere literary exercise but a genuine reflection of life.

As the argument proceeds, we are brought to a fuller realization of the part played by this compelling power in the poet's exercise of his craft. The "working" of the force which, for want of a better word, he calls "Love", the force by which life is driven to its constantly renewed and renewing ends, is indeed "wonderful" in the effects it produces. It is a source of continual admiration in its very unpredictability. Its effects, however, are "sore," acutely painful; and it is here that the two struggles—that of the poet to master his craft and that of the man to realize his creative potentiality through his understanding of "Love"—are most clearly seen in their essential relationship. They leave the poet, poised between affirmation and fear, to meditate—"thynke"—about the state of contradiction in which he finds himself (once again the stress at the end of the line powerfully reinforces the effect), and the upshot of his thinking is to leave him balanced between life and death, achievement and the accompanying sense of continual, *necessary* failure.

In the second stanza the poet—having become aware of the serious, highly contentious nature of what he has just written—turns, very typically, to deprecate himself as one who has very little understanding in these great matters; so, it is insinuated, have in the last analysis, *all* men. His own knowledge, such as it is, has been obtained from his reading, from "bokes." Here, once more, we are touching on the theme of the poet in his relation to "authority," to the achievement of the past. By the very nature of his craft the poet is aware of himself as forming part of a *tradition*, which it is his vocation to restate and interpret for his own time. This is one aspect of the problem, one that confers on the poet's craft seriousness, a sense of vocation; but side by side with and always qualifying it is another sense of the poet as being a theorist, one who is slightly and even absurdly removed in his following of "authority"—written tradition—from direct experience of the living and disturbing truth of "Love," from the sheer reality of what are, marvelously and incomprehensibly, this force's alternations of "miracles" and "cruel ire."

Once more, as throughout the passage, the rhythmic stresses lie unerringly on the key emotions. The introduction is rounded off in a deprecating expression of bewilderment—the sense of helplessness so effectively and so humanly stressed in the final, deliberately simple expression of incapacity. Other poets—Dante supremely among them—can take it upon themselves to reflect a universal vision of the workings in the universe of creative love. Chaucer will be, on occasion, responsive in his own way to these visions, but his poetry will be concerned more with the wayward inconclusiveness of man's distinctively *human* experience. In these opening stanzas of *The Parliament of Fowls* the program that was eventually to come to fruition in *Troilus and Criseyde* and, even more fully, in the design of *The Canterbury Tales* is already insinuated.

All this adds up to a new concept on Chaucer's part of his art and, as a necessary corollary, to a new way of writing in which it may receive expression. The new instrument did not emerge immediately. The *Parliament* turned out, like the poems that preceded it, to be an inadequate vehicle for what the poet had to say; that, no doubt, is why the poem, if not actually broken short like *The House of Fame*, evades any true resolution of the issues it has raised. This is perhaps because Chaucer no longer felt convinced that these issues could be adequately explored in terms of the traditional debate form, and because a dialogue between birds—however witty, varied, and essentially humanized—no longer presented itself to him as a sufficient vehicle for what needed to be said. Not until *Troilus and Criseyde* does Chaucer achieve a rounded and complete poem to answer to the purposes he had in mild—purposes that there, and only there, he at last expresses with full consciousness.

To round off this chapter, and to see where the advances foreshadowed in the *Parliament* could lead, we may consider a passage at the opening of the second canto of *Troilus and Criseyde*. Pandarus's visit to his niece, bringing the news of the love for her that Troilus has declared to him, brings into direct relationship two of the poem's principal characters. The occasion is a suitable one for considering the mature poet's masterful handling of narrative and its "dramatic" possibilities. Chaucer chose for his poem the same intricate and demanding form used in the *Parliament*, the form known in French as *rime roial*, with its elaborate rhyming scheme (ababbcc) and its long, leisurely unit of development. This he combined, though now in notably more fluid form, with the half-line structure and its four stresses that we have already considered. It was his achievement, by so doing, to combine two purposes that perhaps no subsequent English poet has married with the same spontaneity and natural ease. The first of these is the onward flow of narrative, unconstrained by the formal exigencies of rhyme or stanza, smooth, natural, and unhampered in its cumulative effect. The second is the insertion into this narrative progress of an interchange of conversation, easy and colloquial in its kind, projected in a way that tends to the dramatic.

In accordance with this sense of things, Pandarus moves to his objective by stages, in a progress that the movement of the verse reflects. "When he was come . . . to hire folk" (that is, her servants) "quod he": "*And* they hym tolde, *and* he forth in gan pace, / *And* fond. . . ." What he finds at the end of this progress through the antechambers of an aristocratic household is Criseyde sitting with "two othere ladys" in a withdrawn "paved parlour," listening at leisure to the reading of a "geste," the story of another siege—that of Thebes—which constitutes a narrative echo of the real siege of Troy, which is being carried on outside. The siege of Thebes has for these ladies something of the remote, legendary quality that the struggle for Troy has for a reader of Chaucer's own time. It is essentially a "book matter," at once authoritative and distant, serious and conceivably unreal. To his story the ladies listen in a spirit of notable detachment, of passing the time "while hem leste," at their pleasure.

Against this background, quietly and unobtrusively withdrawn, Pandarus delivers his greeting:

> Quod Pandarus, "Madame, God yow see,
> With al youre fayre book and compaignie!"
> "Ey, uncle myn, welcome iwys," quod she;
> And up she roos, and by the hond in hye
> She took hym faste, and seyde, "This nyght thrie,
> To goode mot it turne, of yow I mette."
> And with that word she doun on bench hym sette.
>
> (2. 85–91)

The exchange opens on a note of affectionate politeness, which the easy conversational movement of the verse conveys. The half-line structure is still there, present beneath the flow of the pentameter and ready to be used where the emphasis calls for it; but no longer, as in the *Parliament*, do we feel its presence conditioning our reading, forcing us to recognize its existence. The natural rhythms of speech have taken over in a way that uses structure, or prosody, without stressing it as a separate effect and that allows the dialogue to insert itself into the onward progress of the narrative. Criseyde, as the lady she is, puts the eager, bustling Pandarus at his ease as she introduces him to the secluded company. She also mentions, in passing, the dreams that are, although she is unaware of this, the presagings of a decisive turn in her own fortunes.

Of this turn Pandarus is at this moment the eager harbinger. In his reply and after he has taken up her greeting in a befitting manner, he introduces a note of urgency into the discussion, using the pretext of the book that is being read to introduce the subject that concerns him:

> "But I am sory that I have yow let
> To herken of youre book ye preysen thus.
> For Goddes love, what seith it? telle it us!
> Is it of love? O, som good ye me leere!"
> "Uncle," quod she, "youre maistresse is nat here."
>
> (94–98)

The stressed half-line structure, which has been in abeyance while the poet's main concern was with the development of events, here resumes its place in the stanza. After the easy flow of the first two lines, conveying polite apology, the third line quickens the pace, becomes almost breathless in its effect as Pandarus introduces the purpose of his visit. "For Goddes love," he says with a new note of urgency, "what seith it?"; and, after his question has been stressed by what we must naturally read as a break in the line, he reinforces it with an equally urgent plea—"tell it us"—that stands out by falling into a separate self-contained unit. This serves to introduce the decisive word at which he is aiming in the first half of the next line: "Is it of love?" *Love* is to be the matter of the conversation, as it will be of the whole story; and the phrase stands out again as a stressed and separate unit, admirably completed by the eager and breathless sequel that makes up the second half-line: "O, som good ye me leere!"

The effect does not end here. Criseyde, who knows her uncle and who has full command of the social graces, replies in a deliberately assumed tone of banter, as though to remove any sense of urgency from what has passed or, still more, is to pass between them. "Uncle . . . youre maistresse is nat here." The tone confirms this young widow's ability to keep up her end in the game in which both are engaged (and *know* they are engaged; the effects of the passage are wonderfully varied beneath the appearance of simplicity) in playing. To be noted, here and throughout, is the use of overrunning lines and the clinching of final rhymes in ways that both answer to the natural flow of the dialogue and point to the intended and largely unspoken effects.

At this point and with the social ice broken by her light quip ("With that thei gonnen laugh") Criseyde maintains the tone of the exchange on the level of "romance," distancing the story of Thebes as an insubstantial trifle—"al that dede"—and turning the legendary figure of Amphiorax into a "bishop," even as she casts a note of ironic wit on the authority of the "book" and on the tale of how he—the "bishop"—fell "thorugh the ground to helle." The insertion, at the most telling rhythmical point and in relation to the clinching rhyme, of the phrase "as the book kan telle," is calculated to convey the tone, the poised and skeptical wit, that characterizes this parlor conversation. Perhaps the serious matters—those of "love" and "war"—that are hovering on the edge of this bright talk are best kept at a distance, prevented from erupting dangerously into real life, by being treated in this way. We cannot quite be brought to forget, however, that they are real presences; that the war, with its corollary of doom for Troy, is going on just beyond the walls of this parlor, that the imperious claims of love are the still undisclosed theme of Pandarus's errand, and that both are being treated with a lightness of touch that, attractive though it may be, it will not be possible to maintain. Pandarus will turn out to be too convinced that the course of love lies within his powers of manipulation, Criseyde too ready to forget the circumstances beyond her control by which her fate will be, in fact already is being determined. Beneath the surface of easy, cultivated banter, the foundations of the poem's larger themes are being firmly laid.

This, then, is—paradoxically—the setting in which the dangerous fruits of romance and sentiment flourish. It is a setting in which Pandarus is, or at least feels himself to be, thoroughly at home, as he confirms by the tone of his reply:

> Quod Pandarus, "Al this knowe I myselve,
> And al th'assege of Thebes and the care;
> For herof ben ther maked bookes twelve.
> But lat be this, and telle me how ye fare."
>
> (106–9)

Setting aside these stories as so many "'old wives' tales"—"lat this be": the tone is, once again, unmistakable—Pandarus advances a step farther in his project by challenging his niece to put up her widow's veil: "shewe youre face bare." Let her, in other words, leave her bookish pastimes and the conventions that society imposes on her and do justice to the compulsions of her nature by taking up the "dance" in observance of May: the "dance" appropriate to the season, which answers to the present necessities of life as Pandarus sees them and which reflects nothing less than the immemorial rites of love.[19]

Once again, a sensitive response to the verse and language will tell us that we are at an important turning-point in the story. When Pandarus says "lat be this," or when he adds, with his air of bluff common sense, "Do wey youre barbe" (the widows veil), he is challenging Criseyde to break the ties of custom that unite her to her society: challenging her, in the name of the natural (as he sees "nature," and as we *in part* may see it also), to enter upon an unknown and unpredictably dangerous course. This effect will be obscured if we insist on reading the crucial line as a smooth pentameter, thus:

Do wey youre book, rys up, and lat us daunce,

The real effect, which a natural reading imposes, is rather this:

Do wey youre book, ‖ rys up, │ and lat us daunce,

and it answers to the challenge, the urgency, of a crucial situation. Criseyde is not insensitive to what is being implied. In her reply she takes up her side in the game in which she and her uncle are both (and, by now, both knowingly) engaged. Her part is to protest the propriety of her widowhood, and to express her dread and horror of these unseemly, "wild" proposals:

> "I? God forbede!" quod she, "be ye mad?
> Is that a widewes lif, so God yow save?"
>
> (113–14)

Her proper course (as she puts it, not without a measure of meaningful exaggeration) is to retire from society (to pray "in a cave": the exaggeration of the alternative tells us something about the unreality of what presents itself as a reasonable resolve and is in fact something less consistent and convincing) and to read the lives of "holy seyntes." What Pandarus has proposed is, she says, fitting only for "maydens" and—at best—for "yonge wyves," though, of course, even as we read this, we are meant to reflect that it is with these, rather than with the staid devotees of widowhood, that Criseyde in her youth and beauty naturally belongs.

As always, Chaucer is requiring us to hold a fine and delicate balance. Pandarus has based his appeal on something real in nature—something, we may feel to which a great deal in Chaucer responds—and to it his niece on her side naturally feels attracted; but he is also urging her to set aside obligations that are equally a part of her essentially social, and therefore human nature. Like other great poets, Chaucer was largely concerned with the exploration of the central *crux* represented by the relation of nature to human nature—to ask himself, and to induce us to ask ourselves what it means, specifically and uniquely, to be human. By raising the question in his own way, Pandarus ends by leading Criseyde into uncharted paths of danger.

At this point, and as though emphasizing this, the dialogue quickens as Pandarus moves to the attack:

> "As evere thrive I," quod this Pandarus,
> "Yet koude I telle a thyng to doon yow pleye."
> "Now, uncle deere," quod she, "telle it us
> For Goddes love; is than th'assege aweye?
> I am of Grekes so fered that I deye."
> "Nay, nay," quod he, "as evere mote I thryve,
> It is a thing wel bet than swyche fyve."
>
> "Ye, holy God," quod she, "what thyng is that?
> What! bet than swyche fyve? I! nay, ywys!
> For al this world ne kan I reden what
> It sholde ben; some jape, I trowe, is this;
> And but youreselven telle us what it is,
> My wit is for t'arede it al to leene.
> As help me God, I not nat what ye meene."
>
> "And I youre borugh, ne nevere shal, for me,
> This thyng be told to yow, as mote I thryve!"
> "And whi so, uncle myn? whi so?" quod she.
> "By God," quod he, "that wol I telle as blyve!
> For prouder womman is ther noon on lyve,
> And ye it wist, in al the town of Troye.
> I jape nought, as evere have I joye!"
>
> Tho gan she wondren moore than biforn
> A thousand fold, and down hire eyghen caste;
> For nevere, sith the tyme that she was born,
> To knowe thyng desired she so faste;
> And with a syk she seyde hym atte laste,
> "Now, uncle myn, I nyl yow nought displese,
> Nor axen more that may do yow disese."
>
> (120–47)

Chaucer's art of finely interwoven dialogue—which is, in its very appearance of simplicity, supremely artful—has now reached a stage in which detailed analysis ceases to be appropriate. To respond to the effect it is enough to allow the written words to carry us along with them. What Pandarus is so enticingly offering at this crucial stage in his maneuver is the prospect of "pleye," of light diversion. It is a prospect calculated to move the young widow to lively interest and, of course, it at once does so. "Now, uncle deere," she pleads, not without a note of affectionate urgency; but she is sufficiently in control of herself to turn this eagerness to know what she senses to be behind his words ("For Goddes love") into a suggestion that he may have news of the end of the siege and to stress her womanly fear of the Greeks: "I am of Grekes so fered that I deye." Pandarus, still holding back, offers wider prospects: "It is a thing wel bet than swyche fyve." *Better*, we may reflect, than the end of the war in which the whole of this society, even in the seclusion of this parlor, is involved with ends of life and death. On the surface nothing is stated, nothing emphasized; but it is beginning to be brought home to us that there may be a reversal of proper values involved in Pandarus's manipulations of human motives and feelings.

The end to which these devices will lead is, however, still distant, and for the present he achieves his immediate aim. Criseyde becomes increasingly anxious to hear the news that is being withheld from her. She is realist enough to know that what her uncle proposes is likely to be some kind of "jape," but she is also determined to discover what he has in mind. The dialogue grows more pressing as it moves to the conclusion that Pandarus has foreseen, and for which Criseyde is ready. He continues to tantalize her, while insinuating that the news, if only he cared to declare it, would be a source of pride to her. The result, naturally, is to add to her desire to know what is being kept from her:

> nevere, sith the tyme that she was born,
> To knowe thyng desired she so faste—

but she is sufficiently in control of herself to bide her time, disguising her anxiety and—ostensibly—waiting on her uncle's pleasure.

This passage has been looked at closely, not only because it marks an important stage in the development of the poem, but because it points to some of Chaucer's characteristic virtues. The stanza form that developed from *The Parliament of Fowls* to *Troilus and Criseyde* did not, as it turned out, finally answer to his purposes. These were to find more congenial development in the rhyming couplets of the greater part of *The Canterbury Tales*, where the more elaborate stanza was reserved for matter with a religious, a rhetorical, or, more generally speaking, a certain deliberate, distancing remoteness of effect. The couplets answered more adequately to the needs of the *Tales*. They were more flexible, less constricting in their requirements, and more adapted to the variety of purposes—alternately serious and comic (but where exactly does the border lie in Chaucer?), effective in their narrative progress, endlessly reflecting the conception of life as an inconclusive journey, a pilgrimage that each character interprets in his own way. Just so, we may think, even the solemn, balanced, and spacious design of the *Troilus* poem—where everything is deliberately calculated and disposed, as befits a consciously "great" poem—came to seem too obviously constructed, too final for a poet who tended increasingly to exclude finality from his understanding of human existence. But meanwhile it was no small achievement to have turned the seemingly restrictive pattern of the rhyming scheme he had chosen into an instrument and not, as it might have been, a hindrance to his end, which was already that of displaying human motive and feeling in the process of active development and growing interrelationship. The spoken phrases fall, in their effect of colloquial simplicity, easily and naturally into the pattern of rhythm and stanza, and the rhymes answer with a deceptive air of inevitability to the point that the poet, without undue emphasis or forcing, wishes to underline. Whatever else it may be, this is no naive achievement, produced out of nothing, but rather a distinctive triumph of civilization expressing itself through the voice of a great and highly individual poet approaching the height of his powers.

2
The Book of the Duchess

Chaucer's first poem of recognized individuality has some of the qualities of an occasional piece. Written in 1369, or shortly after, as a kind of "elegy" for Blanche, the first wife of Edward III's brother John of Gaunt, it presented the poet with a considerable challenge as an exercise in literary tact. To address a poem of mingled eulogy and consolation to one of the most prominent men in the realm without appearing either presumptuous or condescending was an undertaking that called for no common sense of discrimination; and to accomplish this while at the same time treating themes that clearly meant a good deal to him was to add another dimension to the achievement. *The Book of the Duchess* shows the poet already engaged in turning the literary models available to him to personal use, embarking on the process of exploration and development that was to lead him to his declared aim of writing poetry in his native language that could stand the test of confrontation with the literary monuments of the classical past.

The subject of the poem is something more than the immediate occasion might suggest. It is *love*; not, however, love romantically or even personally conceived, as a modern writer or a modern reader might view it, but as a recognized subject—perhaps *the* recognized subject—for poetry: a theme that by its very nature raises the deeper issues of human life, particularly the relationship between life (for "love" *is* life, an aspect of the creativity by which men may be said in a true sense to live) and the death that appears to destroy it. Since the poem is an elegy, it is appropriate that this should be its theme; but the immediate occasion should not lead us to ignore the truth that something of more than individual application is being worked out.

In considering the poet's handling of this theme we shall need to consider the sense, explicit and implied, of two words that turn up repeatedly through his work. These two words are *authority* and *experience*, and the exploration of the relationship between them is very close to the heart of the poet's conception. *Authority* is the expression of a consensus of "qualified" opinion on whatever matter may be under discussion. It is, in other words, something rather close to what a modern poet might call "tradition," the product of the accumulated experience of a given society. Chaucer's attitude to this concept, like that of any medieval writer, differs in certain respects from that which any modern author can be expected to have. A medieval writer tended not to think of literary creation in terms of stressed originality or uniquely individual experience; or, if he did (and here we might think of the example of Dante, whose work appears to burst habitually out of this frame of reference with a force of personal emphasis), the fact remains that the "personal" experiences are invariably and—in the case of the real poetry of the age—creatively set against what is assumed to be an objectively valid frame of reference.

For a medieval poet, the proper view on most matters of ultimate human importance had already been worked out outside the literary sphere; this was the purpose of theology, of philosophy, of law, of man's basic speculative and social activities. The poet's task consisted not so much in the attempt to say new things or to convey unique experiences, as in the need to reexpress what was already known (and, in the case of revealed truth at least known for certain) in such a way as to make it live for the present and for succeeding generations. This end the artist achieved through the use of the appropriate devices of his art, which were also the object of explicit formulation based on the study of the recognized models of the past. The idea, it must be stressed, is—in the hands of the real artists of the age—less restrictive than we may think. It recognizes that the theme of poetry is *remembered.* and therefore *past*, experience, which the act of writing recreates in relation to a present reality, a reality, moreover, in which the governing principles on which the poet's society authoritatively rests condition his present understanding of it. The resulting view of poetic creation is, in certain respects, not unlike what T. S. Eliot may have had in mind when he wrote that the writer needed "a sense of the pastness of the past as well as of its presence":[1] needed, in other words, to recognize that each human being *is*, in a very important sense, his own past and that of the humanity to which he belongs: needed to recognize that without some sense of the continuing relevance of the past our present existence could have no content and would cease to be meaningful at all.

This understanding of "tradition" is one side of the picture, which needs, for medieval no less than for modern man, to be balanced by another. *Authority* implies, of its very nature when properly understood, a continual reference back to another constant term in Chaucer's reflections on his art: that summed up in the contrasted or completing term which is *experience*. Awareness of the past as a presence in our lives is necessary and useful, as is the proper respect for tradition, which it implies; but it can only serve our ends inasmuch as it is still alive, and so capable of continuing transformation in the light of our present experience.

Experience, then, tends to be seen in Chaucer as the awareness we have of the present reality of things, which we find is very frequently opposed to a theoretical understanding of the same things as we might think they should be. As such, our interpretations of experience are subject to continual change and development in the process of actual living. Chaucer's work, like that of any real poet in any age, is a continual balance of inherited tradition and direct exposure to life. The terms in which he expresses this understanding are not exactly the same as ours, but they reflect a reality that is permanent beneath changing verbal formulations and philosophies. The tension between the two terms, which makes its first appearance in this poem, is vital for his work. To bridge it, to overcome the gap that he senses in this first considerable poem, Chaucer has recourse to another typically medieval literary device, which he adopted from the French authors at his command, and more particularly from Guillaume de Machaut: the device of the dream.

In *The Book of the Duchess* Chaucer makes use, for the first of many occasions, of the considerable body of medieval speculation, "scientific" and philosophical, on the subject of dreams.[2] The medieval attitude to dreams was in certain respects perhaps more sophisticated than may immediately appear. Very roughly speaking, and with considerable simplification, two kinds of dream are under consideration. There is a distinction between what were sometimes called *somnia naturalia*, "lower" dreams associated with the physical processes of the body, digestive and otherwise, and the "higher" dreams, or *somnia animalia*, based on the operations of the waking mind and rising on occasions to *somnia coelestia*, offering insight into the future and, on occasion, into some aspect of "spiritual" reality.[3] It is the latter kind of dream, offering suggestive analogies with the uncertain but seductive processes of artistic creation, that mainly concerns the sort of literary purpose with which we are here dealing. The poet, like the interpreter of dreams, hopes to find important truths in the process of interpreting his elusive and constantly shifting material; he is aware at the same time of the continual possibility of deception that the very nature of his search implies. Chaucer, like other medieval writers, is apt—especially in his earlier writing—to use dreams to explore a possible reconciliation between the two terms I have already indicated: *authority*, which is apt to present itself under the forms of bookish or academic theory, and the *experience* that derives from the way things actually are.

The poem, then, presents itself initially as a love-vision, reflecting in certain aspects the allegorical French manner. The influence of the *Romaunt of the Rose* and of the work of Machaut is notably strong. At the outset the poet, speaking in the form of the *persona*[4] that he will adopt throughout (this is the first use of a device that he will put to varied use in his later work), declares himself to be in a state of incomprehensible depression. This state, he tells us, proceeds from a lack of sleep, as a result of which

> I have felynge in nothyng,
> But, as yt were, a mased thyng,
> Alway in poynt to falle a-doun;
> For sorwful ymagynacioun
> Ys alway hooly in my mynde.
>
> (11–15)

The condition is recognized to be unnatural—"agaynes kynde"—and in it "melancolye" and "fantasies" prevail in what is evidently a condition of mental and spiritual sickness. Indeed, the poet's state of mind is such as to threaten actual death, for the sufficient reason that

> nature wolde nat suffyse
> To noon erthly creature
> Nat longe tyme to endure
> Withoute slep and be in sorwe.
>
> (18–21)

The unnatural effect of grief as subversive of the normal processes of life, and the means by which a man afflicted by it may be restored to the natural state defined by the "law of kynde" are central themes of the poem.

The poet, initially, declares himself unaware of the cause of his condition. A "sickness" of eight years' duration is mentioned, in terms that are in all probability conventional: the one and only "physician" who is also referred to (39) may be the "lady" of the conventional love poetry or (as some have thought) Christ, the source of the only true healing love. The exact significance remains hidden; what is clear is that the poet, experiencing the reality of an unhappy state, looks for relief to authority in the form of the words written in a book put together in happier times, "While men loved the lawe of kynde" (56): in other words a book that, under the form of a "romaunce," purports to declare the true nature of love. The question raised by implication is that of the trustworthiness of literature, the product of a poet's creative imagination, as a valid reflection of the reality of "love."

The book contains the writings of Ovid, always one of the chief authorities available to a medieval poet in matters of love. The poet turns to the *Metamorphoses* and finds there the tale of Seyx and Alcyone.[5] The story tells how Seyx was drowned during a storm at sea, and how his faithful wife was left disconsolate at his loss. In her grief she regrets that she has been given the gift of life—"'Alas!' quoth shee, 'that I was wrought!'" (90)—for the loss of her husband has made the prospect of continued living intolerable to her. The poet feels intense pity for her sad condition, which he shares as he considers the state into which her sorrow has brought her.

In her grief—to pursue the story as given by Ovid—Alcyone vows herself to the goddess Juno in return for the privilege of seeing her husband again. Juno, in response, sends her messenger to Morpheus, the god of sleep, who is to be found in a sinister and unnatural place, a

> derke valeye
> That stant betwixen roches tweye
> Ther never yet grew corn ne gras,
> Ne tre, ne [nothing] that ought was.
>
> (155–58)

The effect at this point is evidently to present the dream experience as proceeding from an immersion in grief from which, for as long as it remains in exclusive possession of the mourning wife, nothing living or finally valid can be expected. The cave, as a setting for the dream experience, reflects the present state of the dreamer exclusively concentrated upon his loss. It is a sterile place,

> as derk
> As helle-pit overal aboute;
>
> (170–71)

but lest we should be inclined to read too much seriousness into the fable, Chaucer is careful to provide a deflating touch as we are given, in a passage already quoted,[6] the messenger's arrival among the sleepers in the cave.

The deflation, however, indicative though it is of the limitation implied in the tendency of dreams to reflect the immediate state of the dreamer, is not incompatible with a proper sense of the serious issues of life and death. As Morpheus, in the body of Seyx, conveys to Alcyone the message that Juno has inspired, we are aware that what is being stressed is a sober recognition of the reality of death together with an equally sober realization of the uselessness of pursuing grief beyond the limits that nature imposes upon all men in the form of a recognition of their mortal state:

> My swete wyf,
> Awake! let be your sorwful lyf!
> For in your sorwe there lyth no red.
> For, certes, swete, I nam but ded;
>
> (201–4)

Beyond the poignant directness the expression is compatible with a considerable degree of subtlety. Seyx, or his dream-"image" returning from death, calls upon his wife to "awake," to be restored to life from the self-consuming visions of death associated with the dark recesses of the dream-cavern. He speaks with stressed human affection—there is considerable pathos in that simple, effective "swete"—but speaks across the reality of a state that men have no alternative but to accept. In the mere clinging to grief there lies no solution—"no red"—but only a continued dedication to what has become unreal.

"I nam but ded." Seyx's final words carry an essential ambiguity. They stress, on the one hand, the unimportance of the state, the condition of being dead, and on the other, the insignificance, as it may be, of death itself considered as a final reality. "I nam but ded": death—the best authorities, in their wisdom, say—needs to be accepted in a spirit of resignation as an integral and inescapable part of life. This, however, cannot be all the truth, or a truth readily to be accepted. Experience, which is the other side of the equation, tells us that this abstract consolation is far from easy to translate into ordinary human terms, and Alcyone dies in her state of despair. In the lessons offered by authority—moderation in grief and a reasonable acceptance of the inevitable—she "saw noght" (213), and died "within the thridde morwe."

The poet, then, has found no consolation in the content of his reading. What he would still like to achieve is the gift of sleep, and to this end he lists—more or less wittily—the sumptuous gifts that he would be ready to give to Morpheus if only he could be brought to the cave in which, according to the story he has just read, so many gods and spirits were plunged in slumber. This he says in some doubt:

> Me thoghte wonder yf hit were so:
> For I had never herd speke, or tho,
> Of noo goddes that koude make
> Men to slepe, ne for to wake;
>
> (233–36)

for, as he also puts it (and the statement has some reflection on the reliability of the counsel he has obtained from Ovid's tale), "I ne knew never god but oon."

In this mood, quite unexpectedly (the poem plays most effectively on the sense of the unforeseen, the gratuitous, which the dream experience induces) he receives the gift of sleep and dreams

> So wonderful, so ynly swete a sweven,
>
> (276–77)

that no man has ever been vouchsafed the like. The content of the dream, it is suggested, may throw light on, and complete, the insight partly hidden in Ovid's story.

The dream is set in the time of May, the season of love's stirring and the annual rebirth of life. The poet's account of it, and of the bedchamber in which it takes place, is thoroughly literary in its details. It is, after all, the possible value of literature, of the creative imagination, as a source of valid and reasonable consolation that is in question. The "noyse and swetnesse" of the song of the "grete hep" of "smale foules" outside the window; the effect of their harmony as a "moste solempne servise"; the sound, as of invisible instruments ringing through the room with its glazed windows depicting ancient tales of the classical heroes; above all, the fact that

> alle the walles with colours fyne
> Were peynted, bothe text and glose,
> Of al the Romaunce of the Rose:
>
> (332–34)

all these details point to the essentially literary nature of the dream experience we are about to follow. They are intended to contrast with the poet's melancholy condition and the dark secrecy of the cave of Morpheus.

There is, however, more than this to be said. The setting is the background for an experience that moves convincingly in the suspended reality of dream and that concerns the folklore of the hunt:

> And as I lay thus, wonder lowde
> Me thoght I herde an hunte blowe
> T'assay hys horn, and for to knowe
> Whether hyt were clere or hors of soun,
> And I herde goynge, bothe up and doun,

> Men, hors, houndes, and other thyng:
> And al men speken of huntyng,
> How they wolde slee the hert with strengthe.
>
> (344–51)

The hunting of the hart is likely to have carried, for a medieval reader, the sense of a spiritual quest; but, if so, this is not stressed. The emphasis lies on a remarkably vivid evocation of the dream state, a world in which the distinction between the indoor and the outdoor worlds, the poet's chamber and the scene of the hunt merge cunningly into one another:

> Anoon ryght, whan I herde that,
> How that they wolde on-huntynge goon,
> I was ryght glad, and up anoon
> Took my hors, and forth I wente
> Out of my chambre.
>
> (354–58)

It may be easy to read this superficially as naive, childish poetry, but the intention is to create a world suspended from the normal conditions of the real, in which the important issues with which the poem is to be concerned can be developed effectively.

The note of fantasy, indeed, grows even stronger when the dreaming poet draws close to the huntsman and engages him in a conversation in which the laws of waking reality are suspended:

> So at the laste
> I asked oon, ladde a lymere:
> "Say, felowe, who shal hunte here?",
>
> (364–66)

to which the answer, disconcerting in its effect, is: "Syr, th'emperour Octovyen," a revelation that the poet takes disarmingly in his stride: "'A Goddes half, in good tyme!' quod I," and spurs his horse into the hunt: "'Go we faste!' and gan to ryde." We may, if we will, look for allegorical or spiritual meanings in the surprising introduction of the Roman emperor;[7] but it may be closer to the spirit of the whole if we emphasize the folklore quality it shows and ally this to the subtle impression of a mysteriously inconsequent dream world that pervades the whole.

The tone of the poetry, indeed, continues to be abstracted from daily reality. The hunt ends inconclusively with the hart overshot by the pursuing hounds until, again quite unexpectedly, a "whelp" leads the dreamer aside from the chase and induces him to follow it into a world of eternal Spring:

> And I hym folwed, and hyt forth wente
> Doun by a floury grene wente
> Ful thikke of gras, ful softe and swete,
> With floures fele, faire under fete,
> And litel used, hyt semed thus;
> For both Flora and Zephirus,
> They two that make floures growe,
> Had mad her dwellynge ther, I trowe;
> For hit was, on to beholde,
> As thogh the erthe envye wolde
> To be gayer than the heven,
> To have moo floures, swiche seven,
> As in the welken sterres bee.
> Hyt had forgete the povertee
> That wynter, thurgh hys colde morwes,
> Had mad hyt suffre, and his sorwes,
> All was forgeten, and that was sene.
> For al the woode was waxen grene;
> Swetnesse of dew had mad hyt waxe.
>
> (397–415)

The wood, as the following lines show, is not only itself living but full of life; once more, there is a clear implication of contrast with the dark dream-setting of the story of Seyx and Alcyone. This is *nature*, renewed in the springtime after the death of winter, nature as the appropriate setting for love.

In the garden the dreamer finds, not a personification of life and love, but something very different: the sorrowful and withdrawn figure of "a man in blak." The man, quite unaware that he is being observed, proceeds to utter "a compleynt to hymselve,"

> The moste pitee, the moste rowthe,
> That ever I herde.
>
> (465–66)

He shows all the attributes of inconsolable sorrow, and the dreamer expresses great wonder that nature might inspire any creature to such extremity of grief and not lead him "to be ded." On a dream-level, the man in black clearly reflects the content of the Seyx-Alcyone story; there is also a connection with the poet's own unhappy condition as we were told of it at the beginning of the poem. After the actual "compleynt," which is given in eleven lines of the mourner's own words (475–86), from which we learn the actual cause of his sorrow, the lines that follow show all the conventional physical attributes of poetic grief—

> Hys sorwful hert gan faste faynte,
> And his spirites wexen dede;
> The blood was fled for pure drede
> Doun to hys herte, to make hym warm—
>
> (488–91)

and we are told that he has been reduced to a condition that resembles mental alienation, madness.

After this meeting the dreamer and the man in black greet one another in courtly fashion. The mourner apologizes for not having been aware of the dreamer's presence, "Debonayrly, and nothyng lowde" (518); the poet disclaims any thought of resentment—"'A, goode sir, no fors,' quod y"—and presents his excuses for having disturbed the other by his intrusion. Finally, the poet proposes to himself to have "more knowynge of hys thought" (538); since we know that he has already overheard the cause of the mourner's grief, we are to understand that his purpose is less to seek the information that he already has than to draw out the intimate thoughts of his interlocutor with a view, ultimately, of leading him, by allowing open expression to his inner burden of sorrow, to obtain relief from his sad condition. The knight is living—if it can be called living—in the state of mournful abstraction that the nature of his loss seems to impose. Completely unaware of and careless concerning the circumstances of continuing life—the hunt that has just passed, about which he declares that he cares nothing—

> "Y do no fors therof," quod he;
> "My thought ys theron never a del,"
>
> (542–43)

his reaction reflects a condition that, based though it is on the reality of his grief, is against nature and must, if persisted in, lead finally to the loss of life itself.

The knight in black stresses in his reply the unalterable nature of his sorrow. Like Alcyone, he rejects all offer of comfort and declares that it is his wish to die. His expression of his sorrow is both extreme and impossibly self-centred:

> Y wreche, that deth hath mad al naked
> Of al the blysse that ever was maked,
> Yworthe worste of alle wyghtes,
> That hate my dayes and my nyghtes!
> My lyf, my lustes, be me loothe,
> For al welfare and I be wroothe,

> The pure deth ys so ful my foo
> That I wolde deye, hyt wolde not soo;
> For whan I folwe hyt, hit wol flee;
> I wolde have hym, hyt nyl nat me.
>
> (577–86)

"Y am sorwe, and sorwe ys y" (597): the evident pathos of the words, though direct and powerful enough to elicit true sympathy, is none the less the expression of an impossible dedication to grief, a dedication that it will be the poet-dreamer's purpose tactfully to draw into the light of day and—by so doing—to restore the knight himself to the continuing processes of life.

The "compleynt" of the man in black, however, raises issues that are more than merely personal. It culminates in a long indictment of the operations of "false Fortune," by which he feels that he has been betrayed:

> fals Fortune hath pleyd a game
> Atte ches with me, allas the while!
> The trayteresse fals and ful of gyle,
>
> (618–20)

for, as the speaker goes on to recognize, it is the nature of Fortune to deceive those who put their trust in her operations. The knight has committed himself shortsightedly to playing a game of chess with Fortune and has as an inevitable result lost his "fers," the queen piece in the game, and become plunged in the despair in which the dreamer has found him:

> Trowest thou? By oure Lord I wol the seye.
> At the ches with me she gan to pleye;
> With hir false draughtes dyvers
> She staal on me, and tok my fers.
> And whan I sawgh my fers awaye,
> Allas! I kouthe no lenger playe,
> But seyde, "Farewel, swete, ywys,
> And farewel al that ever ther ys!"
>
> (651–58)

The extreme pathos of the expression should not lead us to neglect what is being said. It is the nature of Fortune to be fickle, and the knight admits that, had he been in her place and in possession of her powers, he would have done what she has done. "Had I be God," he says—and the point, of course, lies in the fact that he is not, and cannot be, God—

> Had I be God and myght have do
> My wille, whan she my fers kaughte,
> I wolde have drawe the same draughte.
>
> (680–82)

To "play chess" with Fortune—or, in other words, to challenge her at the level of her own operations—is to face inevitable loss. This, rather than the persistence in despair that led Alcyone to her death, is the real lesson of the Seyx story, now expressed in a different form but finally to the same end. "Death" is an inseparable aspect of the complete process to which we give the name of "life," and as such it has finally to be accepted. As Boethius argued in *De Consolatione Philosophiae* Fortune can only be overcome by those who are able to look beyond the apparent finality of her operations to the Providence that really, if obscurely, controls them.[8]

The knight's error, in fact, lies in a rejection or lacking recognition of the existence and relevance of a provident design in things; and its end is, inevitably and logically, the despair that has led the mourner to desire to die. His loss has been real and his sense of it is properly poignant—after all, he says of Fortune that "she took the beste" (684)—but it should not, on a proper understanding, lead him to the death wish on which his whole being is now concentrated. It will be the purpose of the dreamer, using all his resources of tact and persuasion and proceeding by a gradual process of drawing out, a kind of intimate and progressive confession, to restore the knight to a proper respect for his own being and to a right relationship with the life that in spite of and beyond his immersion in grief, goes on around him.

Any adequate conception of love, indeed, needs to show itself capable of assimilating the reality of death. This is the gist of the consolation, in itself more or less conventional, that the dreamer proceeds to offer and that has already been implied in the Seyx story:

> ther is no man alyve her
> Wolde for a fers make this woo!
>
> (740–41)

This, perhaps, is the best consolation that "authority" can offer a man in the knight's situation; but it is essential to an understanding of Chaucer's purpose in the poem that the victim declares it to be irrelevant to his own case. "Why so?" he replies to the dreamer's attempt to convey the need for resignation,

> hyt is nat soo.
> Thou wost ful lytel what thou menest;
> I have lost more than thow wenest.
>
> (742–44)

The answer points to the inadequacy of all theoretical, generalized consolation in the face of a real, particular loss. The dreamer, who has lost nothing himself, cannot appreciate the true and intolerable nature of another's sorrow. His well-meant consolations fall on the mourner's ear as so many words, theories irrelevant in the face of a unique, and uniquely *personal* situation. It is the presence of this reaction, and the attempt in the rest of the story to overcome it, that gives *The Book of the Duchess* its final interest.

Inspired by his sorrow, and gently persuaded by the dreamer to come out of himself, the knight embarks upon the process of intimate confession that is required for the healing of his state. He begins to tell the story that will explain the full sense and reality of his loss. Looking back on the past, he presents himself in terms established by the courtly convention of love as one dedicated to the "service" of his lady:

> "Syr," quod he, "sith first I kouthe
> Have any maner wyt fro youthe,
> Or kyndely understondyng
> To comprehende, in any thyng,
> What love was, in myn owne wyt,
> Dredeles, I have ever yit
> Be tributarye and yiven rente
> To Love, hooly with good entente,
> And throgh plesaunce become his thral
> With good wille, body, hert, and al.
> Al this I putte in his servage,
> As to my lord, and dide homage;
> And ful devoutly I prayed hym to,
> He shulde besette myn herte so
> That hyt plesaunce to hym were,
> And worship to my lady dere.
>
> (759–74)

The knight stresses that the process of his dedication was a result of his growth in "kyndely understondyng," in maturing recognition of his "kyndely," or naturally human nature. To love is to grasp and further the bonds of relationship to one's fellows in which human life, in the deepest sense, properly consists.

Prompted by this understanding, the knight came to seek an object of his dedication, a recognition of the force of love as an essential impulse, bonding and vivifying, in human life. He affirms that the impulse to love is one that men and women cannot deny without doing violence to their natures:

> And this was longe, and many a yer,
> Or that myn herte was set owher,

> That I dide thus, and nyste why;
> I trowe hit cam me kyndely.
> Paraunter I was therto most able,
> As a whit wal or a table,
> For hit is redy to cacche and take
> Al that men wil theryn make,
> Whethir so men wil portreye or peynte,
> Be the werkes never so queynte.
>
> (775–84)

The stress lies on the natural, spontaneous growth of love as a force in life (it "cam me *kyndely,*" by "kind," the speaker says), as well as on the varied forms in which men interpret it in the light of their own individual natures. Human nature in this sense is to be likened to a "white wall" or a "table"—a "tablet" or, as we might say, a painter's canvas: a plain surface on which, in the course of our existence, we paint our own designs following whatever sense we may have of the meaning of our several lives. The emphasis rests, in a very Chaucerian way, on each individual's personal and subjective experience, which confers "value" upon what is of itself a blank surface waiting to be worked upon; that the resulting product may be "queynt," strange, difficult, or perversely contradictory, is implied in the very nature of the experience. It is further emphasized in what follows that this early dedication to the "service" of love is something that came to the speaker in the time of his youth, when he lived in "idleness" and when his achievements—his "works"—were still unconsolidated, "flyttynge" (801) and unstable:

> Al were to me ylyche good
> That I knew thoo.
>
> (803–4)

The fixing of vague and generalized aspirations on a particular and worthy object of devotion, and the separation of that object from others by virtue of the value that the imagination confers upon it, is seen to mark the passage from adolescent devotion to conscious maturity.

What immediately follows—the knight's account of the occasion of his first succumbing to love—is given once more in terms consecrated by literary tradition. Among a company of ladies he saw the object of his devotion and was, in the manner of courtly lovers, immediately dedicated to her service:

> she ful sone, in my thoght,
> As helpe me God, so was ykaught
> So sodeynly, that I ne tok
> No maner counseyl but at hir lok

> And at myn herte; for-why hir eyen
> So gladly, I trow, myn herte seyen,
> That purely tho myn owne thoght
> Seyde hit were beter serve hir for noght
> Than with another to be wel.
>
> (837–45)

The terms of this devotion are familiar and, in certain respects, limiting. The emphasis rests on the "heart," on an irresistible force of sentiment; and there is at least the suggestion that reason has little or no part to play in this situation. The actual description confirms this impression. The lady, as described by her admirer, has all the perfections—physical and spiritual—normally attributed to the courtly mistress. She was, in his eyes, "The soleyn fenix of Arabye" (982), and stress is laid on her possession of the supreme quality of "trouthe":[9]

> Trouthe hymself, over al and al
> Had chose hys maner principal
> In hir, that was his restyng place.
>
> (1003–5)

At the end, the lover declares that she was

> My suffisaunce, my lust, my lyf,
> Myn hap, myn hele, and al my blesse,
> My worldes welfare, and my goddesse.
>
> (1038–40)

Such language represents at once a true fulfillment of courtly love and its final insufficiency; for it remains true that perfection of this kind is not, and cannot be on Fortune's terms, immortal, and that its end can only, on these terms, lie in death.

It is important to see here the direction that Chaucer's thought is taking. Like Dante in the *Vita Nuova* he is arguing, not certainly that love is simply a deception (for the very terms of its expression by the knight presents it as a source of life), but that any conception of it that fails to come to terms with the reality of human mortality is destined to end in disappointment. So the best authorities available to the poet have consistently said, and he is ready to accept the truth of what they say; but between the generality of the statement and its realization in experience—which is still, as always, the other term in the equation—there is, equally necessarily and truly, a gap that can only be filled with difficulty. The pain of loss in such a situation is a reality that cannot be ignored or theoretically resolved.

Throughout this time we have been moving steadily toward the conclusion of the story: a conclusion that we (and the poet-dreamer) already know, but that the sorrowing knight has to be brought to declare through what amounts to a painful experience of confession. The conclusion begins to emerge when the dreamer, commenting on what he has just heard, concludes that the knight believed that his lady was the best of all conceivable objects of devotion. The dialogue at this point acquires a certain tone of urgency:

> "By oure Lord," quod I, "y trowe yow wel!
> Hardely, your love was wel beset;
> I not how ye myghte have do bet."
> "Bet? ne no wyght so wel," quod he.
> "Y trowe hyt, sir," quod I, "parde!"
> "Nay, leve hyt wel!" "Sire, so do I;
> I leve yow wel, that trewely
> Yow thoghte that she was the beste."
>
> (1042–49)

What is insinuated here is a possible discrepancy between what the lover thought—and needed to believe, as a condition of his love—and what might, on a more dispassionate reasoning, be the truth. The terms of the discussion are not, of course, to be simplified so as to impose an easy moralizing conclusion. The poem is dealing not with abstractions, but with the working out of actual, lived experience. The grief-stricken lover remembers the unique, transforming quality of his emotion and concludes, not only that it would *seem* impossible to do other or better (as the dreamer recognizes), but that it *was so*: that his love included within its terms the sum of all possible fulfillment. The dreamer, genuinely moved by what he has heard, recognizes the force of this; but since he is not a protagonist but an observer, and can therefore see things as in some sense they are, he can emphasize the subjective element in the knight's attitude, insisting that it was in his own thought that his love constituted the best of all conceivable realities.

Drawn out in this way by the dreamer's probings, the knight goes on to describe the course of his wooing. His account amounts to a recapitulation of the love process prescribed by familiar conventions, and it moves steadily to a conclusion that is still being held back from us. He begins by recalling the ardor, and the necessary inexperience of his first devotion:

> I was ryght yong, soth to say,
> And ful gret nede I hadde to lerne.
>
> (1090–91)

His love, as he recalls it, seemed to him sufficient to relieve him from all grief and sorrow: "Me thoghte nothyng myghte me greve" (1106). The dreamer, however, moved by his own kind of experience, is unable to accept this as the last word. He reacts with the moralizing comment that joy of this kind contains an element of illusion:

> "Me thynketh ye have such a chaunce
> As shryfte wythoute repentaunce."
>
> (1113–4)

The knight, he says, seems to be in the illogical position of a man who desires to receive in the accustomed forms of the Church absolution for sins committed without going through the necessary preliminary of repentance. He seems to aspire to the end of happiness without passing through a recognition of the necessary limits of all merely human and temporal satisfaction.

The knight, however, is unable to see things in this way. As he puts it, taking up the dreamer's own terms in the process of repudiating his conclusion,

> "Repentaunce! nay, fy!" quod he,
> "Shulde y now repente me
> To love?",
>
> (1115–17)

and goes on to associate such an attitude with some of the most familiar examples of betrayal in the classical tradition. Once again we should not underestimate the force of his objection. He sees love as a force of life and regards this moralizing judgment as nothing less than a refusal to live. The two attitudes are, at this point, delicately balanced against one another; they will need to be pulled together, in some sense harmonized, before the poem ends, but the resolution will not be arrived at by a process of abstract manipulation, or simply by ignoring one term in the complete equation to advance the other. In reply to his interlocutor the knight sums up his attitude by asserting that he will *never* allow the object of his devotion to pass from his grieving mind and heart:

> Nay, while I am alyve her,
> I nyl foryete hir never moo;
>
> (1124–25)

and, although there is an implicit recognition of the transitory in his phrase, "while I am alyve her," the validity of the statement is such as to affirm its relevance in the complete conception.

Proceeding with his narrative, and at the poet's carefully introduced request (he is carrying out his purpose, which is to be a kind of lay confessor who aims at unburdening the other of his sorrow), the knight recalls how his love passed from the first stage of distant adoration enjoined by all the conventions to a first exchange with the object of his devotion. He also leads him, beyond this, to a declaration of what he has lost, without however yet arriving at any explicit statement:

> "Yee!" seyde he, "thow nost what thow menest:
> I have lost more than thou wenest."
>
> (1137–38)

The implication is that the dreamer's moralizing attitudes have still to be tested in relation to the intolerable facts of a sorrowing situation, a loss such that no theory can adequately deal with it.

The dreamer, meanwhile, pursues his intention, which is to lead the knight to an open declaration of the reality of his loss. The real cause of grief has to be declared, brought out into the open, before the process of healing can begin to take shape. The approach to the conclusion is very skillfully modulated, so as to combine the tact required to offer consolation in a situation of no small social delicacy with the deeper purposes of the poem. The narrator, pretending to misunderstand, or at least to ignore the real thrust of what he has heard, insinuates the possibility that the knight may be mourning the desertion of his love. In response, the knight tells him how he pressed his devotion (following the conventional forms) indirectly, without proceeding to any open statement. He recalls how he found himself torn between the insistent need to declare his love and his fear of being rejected, until, at last, encouraged by the thought of his lady's perfections, he arrived at a declaration of his devotion and begged for her "mercy." The declaration was made in the recognition of unworthiness that the convention imposed:

> Ful ofte I wex bothe pale and red.
> Bowynge to hir, I heng the hed;
> I durst nat ones loke hir on,
> For wit, maner, and al was goon.
> I seyde "mercy!" and no more.
>
> (1215–19)

It led to a statement on the part of the lover that he would be "stedfaste and trewe," entirely devoted, and that she represented the totality of his human aspirations:

> I swor hir this—
> "For youres is alle that ever ther ys
> For evermore, myn herte swete!

> And never to false yow, but I mete,
> I nyl, as wys God helpe me soo!"
>
> (1231–35)

There is about this assertion something forced, exaggerated in relation to any possible facts, any conceivable human reality. Of no creature can it reasonably be said "youres is alle that ever ther ys." To say so much is to invite disillusionment, to seek to found a human relationship (which is good just insofar as it remains human) upon a basis of inhuman abstraction and evasion of the real.

This, no doubt, is why in the next stage of the knight's story, the lady, far from going along with these excesses, turns away from her "servant" in no uncertain manner. As the knight puts it, mingling his own ruefulness with Chaucer's unmistakably personal note of humor:

> And whan I had my tale y-doo,
> God wot, she acounted nat a stree
> Of al my tale, so thoghte me.
> To telle shortly ryght as hyt ys,
> Trewly hir answere hyt was this;
> I kan not now wel counterfete
> Hir wordes, but this was the grete
> Of hir answere; she sayde 'nay'
> Al outerly.
>
> (1236–44)

The reply in itself is, of course, consistent with what the conventions demanded. The lady was expected, initially, to show disdain to her "servant"; but there is little doubt that here, beyond the dictates of convention, the poet is advancing the purposes of his story, which include a recognition of the need for *any* human emotion, including "love," potentially the most valuable of them all, to come to terms with the reality in relation to which it has, inescapably and finally positively, to be lived. We can relevantly compare the lady's reaction to the refusal of Beatrice, in Dante's *Vita Nuova*,[10] to respond to the poet's expectation of a response to his devotion.

The lady's rejection is not, in Chaucer's poem, the end of the story; nor, as in Dante's conception, does the knight have to recognize his insufficiency and accept the reality of his mistress's death before he can be reunited to her. Chaucer, working within a frame of reference that he shares with Dante, shows himself to be a different kind of poet. In the long run, and in the knight's story, the human reality of love prevailed. His lady accepted his devotion, still in terms of the love convention—she gave him "The noble yifte of hir mercy," but always "Savynge hir worship" (1269–71)—and they were united in a fulfillment that lasted "ful many a yere":

> Therwyth she was alway so trewe,
> Our joye was ever ylyche newe;
> Oure hertes wern so evene a payre,
> That never nas that oon contrayre
> To that other, for no woo.
> For sothe, ylyche they suffred thoo
> Oo blysse, and eke oo sorwe bothe;
> Ylyche they were bothe glad and wrothe;
> Al was us oon, withoute were.
>
> (1287–95)

This is the bliss to which human beings may reasonably aspire, the hope that they may seek, in the measure of the humanly possible, to achieve. It is, while it lasts, real; real, at least, with the reality that an aspiration may properly have and that it may in some measure confer upon the actual; but it is not, and of its human nature cannot be, finally permanent, and this the conclusion of the knight's story brings out, as he declares the true ground of his sorrow.

This conclusion is at last revealed with a considerable degree of artistic tact. Moved by the emotional quality of the knight's story, and anticipating what has still to be told, the dreamer senses that the time has come to set his interlocutor before the reality of his situation. What follows is given with remarkable delicacy and respect for the reality of grief:

> "Sir," quod I, "where is she now?"
> "Now?" quod he, and stynte anoon.
> Therwith he wax as ded as stoon,
> And seyde, "Allas, that I was bore!
> That was the los that here before
> I tolde the that I hadde lorn.
> Bethenke how I seyde here-beforn,
> 'Thow wost ful lytel what thow menest;
> I have lost more than thow wenest'—
> God wot, allas! ryght that was she!"
> "Allas, sir, how? what may that be?"
> "She ys ded!" "Nay!" "Yis, be my trouthe!"
> "Is that youre los? Be God, hyt ys routhe!"
>
> (1298–1310)

The revelation is as delicate as it is humanly true. The knight has lost his lady beyond recovery. "She ys ded," as he quite simply puts it, and the revelation of the truth unites the story to the implications of Seyx's words to Alcyone when he appeared to her after his death and enjoined on her the need for resignation in the face of a specifically human reality. The dreamer, now obliged to feel the insufficiency, beyond a certain point, of all his theories in the face of the real fact of bereavement, can only offer his "routhe," his distinctively human compassion: "Is that youre los? Be God, hyt is routhe!"

The closing lines of the poem, following on this "revelation," are inconclusive in a way that is very typically Chaucerian: inconclusive, evasive of final resolutions, without being in any way indefinite or dishonest. Neither authority, moral precept enshrined in tradition, nor experience, recognition of things as they are, can have the last word in this debate, because, if the first is necessary, indispensable to a proper understanding of life, the second will always, and necessarily, tend to bring it back to the finally intractable nature of given reality. A complete view of love—which implies nothing less than a balanced attitude to the whole of life, in which what we call love occupies a central and uniquely creative place—will need to take the reality of death into account. To fail to do this, or to evade consideration of death as a fact, is to surrender to illusion and to end in a necessarily bitter awakening; but this moralizing conclusion has equally to recognize that the loss that death brings with it is a *real* loss, and no amount of theory (not even of the best and most respected theory) can diminish the reality of the pain that the loss, in human terms, involves.

Meanwhile the hunt, from which this dream-conversation began by abstracting itself, is finally over. The king (perhaps Christ, who hunts the "hart" that is the human soul? We shall do well not to press the echo too far, but it may be there) has gone back to the castle on the hill with its "walles white" (1318)—possibly an evocation of the "heavenly Jerusalem," where alone true and lasting felicity lies—and the poet is left with the book containing the story of Seyx and Alcyone, which he was reading at the beginning of his story—left also with the memory of his dream, to continue in his task of working out the compromise between the ideal and the real that is perhaps, as he sees it, the essence of human life.

3
The House of Fame

The House of Fame, though written later than *The Book of the Duchess*, may seem a less immediately attractive work. Part of the problem it raises is the result of its unfinished state. We do not know precisely how—or, indeed, if—Chaucer intended to finish it. A certain quality of open-endedness, the avoidance of conclusions that may appear at once definite and limiting, is at all times a characteristic feature of his work. As it stands, the poem clearly shows the same tendency to play off against one another for creative ends the three themes—those of authority, of experience, and of the love-vision—that we found in the previous poem. The concern is now more directly with the meaning of literary creation. The poet is considering, for the first of many times in his work, the nature and the limitation of his vocation.

The poem opens with a somewhat extended *Proem*, or introduction (1–65), which is followed by a further invocation (66–110). Chaucer at once introduces the subject of dreams, always associated in his mind with the processes of imaginative creation, but is notably evasive regarding their possible significance. Is there truth, he seems to ask, in the claim that dreams—like poems—can offer insight into the reality of things, albeit "too darkly" (51)? On this difficult matter, concerning which "grete clerkys" have expressed themselves at length—and, it is implied, with notable contradiction—the poet declares himself as having "noon opinion" (55): a noncommittal position, which he supports by invoking good upon those who are receptive to what he has to say and ill upon those who may "misdeme," or misinterpret it. The general effect is to qualify any serious implications that the example of earlier poets and "authorities" may lend to the matter of his poem and to prepare the way for the very personal note of comic detachment that will prevail throughout its course.

Having disposed of his introduction, the poet embarks upon his account of a dream that came to him while resting on a pilgrimage to the "corseynt" (117)—the holy body—of St. Leonard, who was held to be the patron of those in captivity and might therefore be invoked by those who find themselves in a "prison." The captivity may be that of "love" in general or—in view of more specific references to come—of the married state. In either case the poet dreamed that he found himself in the temple of the goddess Venus, whose image appeared to him "Naked fletynge in a see" (133),[1] and in the company of her "doves," of her blind son "daun Cupido" (137), and of "Vulcano" (138), who—we are intended to remember—was responsible for the punishment inflicted on herself and Mars for their relationship. This is evidently the ambiguous force of desire so frequently associated with Venus in medieval poetry and here treated in a notably unsolemn mood of comic detachment.

The substance of the dream, which occupies the next 327 lines, is a very selective summary of the principal matter of Vergil's *Aeneid*. The emphasis rests not on the "providential" adventures of the founder of Rome, but on the part played in these by Aeneas's mother, the very goddess Venus in whose "temple" the poet is experiencing his dream. After a few lines that repeat in translation the opening of the *Aeneid*, the fall of Troy is briefly remembered, with the attention focused on the intervention of Venus to save her son. Aeneas's adventures are then rather baldly summarized until the point is reached when he meets his goddess-mother, who sends him on his way to Carthage.

It is here, evidently, that the main emphasis in this retelling of the epic story is to rest. Aeneas is of interest to Chaucer not primarily as a "hero" engaged in a divinely sponsored mission, but as a lover, though it should also be noted that the poet is careful to avoid the more romantic implications of his theme, and that he expressly declares that he is without experience in these matters:

> What shulde I speke more queynte,
> Or peyne me my wordes peynte
> To speke of love? Hyt wol not be;
> I kan not of that faculte.
>
> (245–48)

To tell the whole story, moreover, would be "a long proces to telle" (251) and one that holds out no small prospect of becoming tedious. This is a theme that will be constant in Chaucer and that will be given notable expression, for example, in the treatment of the narrator in *Troilus and Criseyde*, whose incapacity in matters of "love" becomes an essential part of the total effect made by the poem. The device is one that Chaucer repeatedly uses to distance himself (and, by implication, his readers) from his material, more especially when the incongruous matter of "love"—which can be alternately tragic and comic, serious and absurd—is in question.

The story of Dido and Aeneas had, of course, an enormous resonance for the medieval imagination. It raised the fundamental question of the relationship to the rest of life of that powerful and ambivalent force that we can call desire, and that, again for the medieval mind, was associated with the powers of Venus: Venus as source of alternating life and death, raising men and women to the heights of creative experience and leading them ruthlessly to destruction. For some great poets—notably Dante, in the Paolo and Francesca episode of the *Inferno*[2] and elsewhere in the *Commedia*—this was a theme of high seriousness, closely connected with man's essential nature; and if Chaucer chose deliberately here to subject it to the play of his comic irony, the finally serious implication remains none the less valid. As the poem passes from the bald summary of Aeneas's adventures to dwell on this central episode, we are told how Dido surrendered herself to her Trojan lover, how she

>   Made of hym shortly at oo word
>   Hyr lyf, hir love, hir lust, hir lord.
>   (257–58)

This is the heart of the story, as this poet chooses to tell it; and it is noteworthy that the stress is placed emphatically, not on the heroic aspect of Aeneas's adventures, but on his treachery to Dido, on the difference between the way in which he presented himself to her and the baser reality of his motivation. Dido, we are told,

>   dide hym al the reverence,
>   And leyde on hym al the dispence,
>   That any woman myghte do,
>   Wenynge hyt had al be so
>   As he hir swor; and herby demed
>   That he was good, for he such semed.
>   (259–64)

The emphasis is placed, as it will be so often in Chaucer's work, on the difference between what "seems" and what "is"; and the results for Dido were disastrous:

>   Allas! what harm doth apparence,
>   Whan hit is fals in existence!

> For he to hir a traytour was;
> Wherfore she slow hirself, allas!
>
> (265-68)

Dido's error lay in the misplaced trust that led her to "love him that unknowen ys" (270). A lesson more different from that implied in Vergil's reading of the story, where Dido's passion is seen as a temptation drawing the hero from the fulfillment of his vocation, would be hard to imagine.

The emphasis in Chaucer's version is placed, then, squarely upon betrayal, which is seen as a universal male attribute:

> For this shall every woman fynde,
> That som man, of his pure kynde,
> Wol shewen outward the fayreste,
> Tyl he have caught that what him leste;
> And thanne wol he causes fynde,
> And swere how that she ys unkynde,
> Or fals, or privy, or double was.
>
> (279-85)

Dido's lament takes up and develops this theme of masculine faithlessness. Can it be, she asks rhetorically, that *every* man is

> thus trewe,
> That every yer wolde have a newe?
>
> (301-2)

Can it be that *all* men are moved to take women either for fame, "In magnyfyinge of hys name" (306), for what is called "frendshippe," or for either "delyt" or "synguler"—that is, particular, selfish—"profyt" (310)? The raising of these questions leads Dido to doubt the existence of any truth in the eloquence that men so readily show in the pursuit of their desires:

> O, have ye men such godlyhede
> In speche, and never a del of trouthe?
>
> (330-31)

where "trouthe" is already beginning to assume its essential Chaucerian meaning of "trust" as the basis of all valid human relationship.[3] The poet, having allowed Dido to express herself in this pathetic manner, is in turn careful to point out that all her "compleynt" and "moon,"

> Certeyn, avayleth hir not a stre.
>
> (363)

Dido killed herself in her despair, and Chaucer supports her tragedy at some length by citing all the familiar bookish examples of masculine infidelity; though it is true that Aeneas is somewhat perfunctorily separated from these discreditable parallels—the "boke seyth," as the poem has it—by the recognition of the providential mission that led him to follow his path to Italy.

At the end of his dream, the poet appears to be in something of a quandary with respect to his attitude toward love. Leaving the Temple of Venus in the hope of finding someone "That may telle me where I am" (479), he finds himself—still in his dream—in a barren desert, which may answer to his own disoriented state:

> When I out at the dores cam,
> I faste aboute me beheld.
> Then sawgh I but a large feld,
> As fer as that I myghte see,
> Withouten toun, or hous, or tree,
> Or bush, or grass, or eryd lond;
> For al the feld nas but of sond
> As smal as man may se yet lye
> In the desert of Lybye;
> Ne no maner creature
> That ys yformed be Nature
> Ne sawgh I, me to rede or wisse.
>
> (480–91)

Faced by this prospect, feeling himself lost and isolated from any contact with the life of "nature," he prays—and prays in an explicitly Christian sense—for deliverance:

> "O Crist!" thoughte I, "that art in blysse,
> Fro fantome and illusion
> Me save!"
>
> (492–94)

He prays, in other words, to be delivered from the world of illusory deception, the "illusions" of Love and Fame so disconcertingly and even absurdly presented to him in his Vergilian dream.[4] In answer to his mockingly anguished prayer, an eagle descends, of surpassing splendor:

> That never sawe men such a syghte,
> But yf the heven had ywonne
> Al newe of gold another sonne:
>
> (504–6)

The House of Fame   59

an eagle that recalls the one that appeared to Dante in his dream to carry him from ante-Purgatory to the place of purgation proper.[5] Following this illustrious precedent, Chaucer is about to be taken up to heaven: taken, however, in the very different spirit and to the highly diverse ends that his comic purpose demands.

By the end of the First Book, two things have become clear. The poet's view of *love*—whatever the word may be held to imply—has been a disillusioning one, and "authority," in the shape of his dream of Vergil's story of Dido, has confirmed this impression. It now remains to be seen to what new "tidings" of love the eagle will bear the poet: and, moreover, whether these tidings will be such as to throw some positive light on this intractable subject.

It is immediately apparent that this eagle, in spite of the impressive way in which it entered the poem, is a very different kind of bird from the one that appeared to Dante in his dream in Purgatory. There the eagle had borne the poet to lofty, if dangerous heights, and the poet, on his part, had been made conscious of his unique vocation. Here the poet is an unwilling and somewhat ridiculous passenger in the grasp of the bird that has seized the diffident author—"Me, fleynge, *in a swap* he hente" (543): the deliberately unpoetic language stresses the indignity to which the dreamer is being subjected—and that bears him upward, not like the Jovian eagle soaring aloft with Ganymede in his talons, but "As lyghtly as I were a larke" (546). The eagle, moreover, addresses its burden in very human terms:

> he to me spak
> In mannes vois, and seyde, "Awak!
> And be not agast so, for shame!"
> (555–57)

and its tone is reminiscent—if not of the poet's own wife, as some writers have perhaps too obviously proposed—of tones familiar to him in everyday life:

> "Awak," to me he seyde,
> Ryght in the same vois and stevene
> That useth oon I koude nevene;
> And with that vois, soth for to seyn,
> My mynde cam to me ageyn,
> For hyt was goodly seyd to me,
> So nas hyt never wont to be.
> (560–66)

At this point, and throughout what follows, the original Dantesque reference to the eagle of *Purgatorio* 9 seems to be extended to cover the further ascent of Dante under the guise of Beatrice, a stern and sometimes reproving moral and intellectual tutor, in the *Paradiso*.[6] Whatever the exact sense, these mundane comparisons seem to place the whole episode in a very un-Dantesque context, one that evidently answers to the poet's essentially comic intention.

The eagle, indeed, soon allows it to be seen that it is bored with carrying this unwilling burden and sees no reason for doing so:

> Seynte Marye!
> Thou art noyous for to carye,
> And nothyng nedeth it, pardee!
>
> (573–75)

Chaucer, on his side, presents himself as thoroughly afraid for his life and with no wish to be "stellified"; the Dantesque and "paradisal" reverberation of the word is evident. When he says "I neyther am Ennok, ne Elye" (588), the echo of Dante is indeed explicit.[7] The eagle makes it clear that the poet's unwilling ascension has nothing to do with any merit on his part. Jupiter, it tells him, has taken pity on him because he has so long, so "trewely" and "ententyfly" (attentively) served the goddess Venus and her blind son, and this without receiving any reward—"Withoute guerdon ever yit" (619)—and although his wit is little, "in thy hed ful lyte is" (621). The eagle's words amount to a gentle but pervasive satire on Chaucer's own practices as a poet whose persistent, but somewhat pitiful aim it has always been

> To make bookys, songes, dytees,
> In ryme, or elles in cadence,
> As thou best canst, in reverence
> Of Love, and of hys servantes eke,
> That have hys servyse soght, and seke;
> And peynest the to preyse hys art,
> Although thou haddest never part;
> Wherfore, also God me blesse,
> Jove halt hyt gret humblesse,
> And vertu eke, that thou wolt make
> A-nyght ful ofte thyn hed to ake
> In thy studye, so thou writest,
> And ever mo of love enditest,
> In honour of hym and in preysynges,
> And in his folkes furtherynges,
> And in hir matere al devisest,
> And noght hym nor his folk dispisest,

> Although thou maist goo in the daunce
> Of hem that hym lyst not avaunce.
>
> (622-40)

The comic tone should not obscure from us that Chaucer is here introducing the real subject of his poem: a consideration of his own talents, and of the kind of poet he wished to be. Thus far, it seems, he has followed the normal conventions, which have prescribed Love and its "service" as the proper theme for writing in verse; but though he has devoted himself to this purpose, writing endlessly in his "study"—and turning himself, it could be said, into an academic writer, who works at a remove from what he knows to be the real—the results have been discouraging. Having incorporated himself into the "dance," he finds himself without "advancement" in its pursuit; the reference is at least as much to his lack of achievement as a poet as it can be to his success as a lover. We shall not understand properly either this passage or a great deal of medieval verse unless we see that these two apparently separate subjects of "love" and "poetry" are in fact largely one and inseparable. To "love" is, in poetic terms, to "create," and what Chaucer is calling into question is his relationship to the literary convention in which he finds himself and which, as he now sees, does not answer to the needs, as yet largely undefined, of his developing genius.

The following lines confirm this, still within the terms of the poet's comic intention. Addressing the author, helplessly borne aloft in its claws, the eagle tells him ("beau sir"; the comic urbanity of the address is typical) "other," and not particularly flattering "thynges." It draws in fact a thoroughly absurd picture of Chaucer's practice as the most bookish of writers:

> thou hast no tydynges
> Of Loves folk yf they be glade,
> Ne of noght elles that God made;
> And noght oonly fro fer contree
> That ther no tydynge cometh to thee,
> But of thy verray neyghebores,
> That duellen almost at thy dores,
> Thou herist neyther that ne this;
> For when thy labour doon al ys,
> And hast mad alle thy rekenynges,
> In stede of reste and newe thynges,
> Thou goost hom to thy hous anoon;
> And, also domb as any stoon,
> Thou sittest at another book

> Tyl fully daswed ys thy look,
> And lyvest thus as an heremyte,
> Although thyn abstynence ys lyte.
>
> (644–60)

The poet's artistic efforts are presented as a continuation of his public function. Both involve a poring upon books and "reckonings," and both imply an exclusion of "new things," a devotion to what is dead and unrewarding at the expense of what is genuinely alive. To be a poet in this way by candlelight is not much more than the continuation of being a civil servant—a bureaucrat, we would now say—by day. Both are in substance a kind of "hermit," though without the dedication to a spiritual end that inspires the abstinence of the latter. Both are denying the claims of life and making their own fulfillment, either as men or as poets, impossible. Beneath the note of wry, personal deprecation, the poet is raising basically serious questions about the conception of the art to which he has so far devoted himself and about the relationship of this conception to the actual business of living.

Having made clear these matters, the bird goes on to inform its passenger of his ultimate destination, which is to be the House of Fame. There, it stresses, the inconstancy of love and its unpredictable nature will be made apparent. The effect is to leave the poet lost in confusion. When the eagle, interrupting its exposition, asks him if he has been able to follow all this, he confesses his bewilderment:

> "Unnethe maistow trowen this?"
> Quod he. "Noo, helpe me God so wys!"
> Quod I. "Noo? why?" quod he. "For hyt
> Were impossible, to my wit,
> Though that Fame had alle the pies
> In al a realme, and alle the spies,
> How that yet she shulde here al this."
>
> (699–705)

Once again the stress is on the intractable, contradictory nature of the material under discussion. The bird, however, is not discouraged. "O yis, yis!" it asserts confidently, in answer to the doubts expressed by the poet, and goes on to state its ability to offer rational "preve" (707) of what it has just asserted.

There follows (765–822) a long explanation by the eagle, in deliberately "scientific" terms, of the way in which the discordant voices of human beings reach their final destination in the House of Fame. The passage is an admirable piece of clear exposition, which shows Chaucer doing in terms of English poetry something of what Dante had so successfully achieved in Italian: making the language and verse of the vernacular capable of expressing itself convincingly on "serious" subjects hitherto considered to be beyond its range. Like Dante, Chaucer expresses himself through the bird's voice as properly proud of his achievement; but the bird's voice, in part because it comes from a bird, strikes us—unlike that of Dante—as notably comic in its inflection, and there is a strong sense of this academic exponent taking pleasure in the definitive quality, as it sees it, of its exposition.[8]

When the bird challenges the poet to agree that the "proof" has been thorough, simple, and exhaustive, his response is suitably submissive: "And y answered and seyde, 'Yis.'" (864). The recognition moves the eagle to an emphatic and deliciously comic display of academic self-approval:

> "A ha!" quod he, "lo, so I can
> Lewedly to a lewed man
> Speke, and shewe hym swyche skiles
> That he may shake hem be the biles,
> So palpable they shulden be."
>
> (865–69)

The bird-lecturer is clearly asking to be flattered for the clarity of its explanation, addressed to "lewd," unlettered men—such as the poet may be thought to be—and so plainly delivered as to be capable of being "shaken by the bills." Like others of its kind, it does not willingly vacate its platform. It goes on to announce its intention of taking the entire subject quite as far as it will go; and this, whether the hearer will or no:

> "Be God," quod he, "and as I leve,
> Thou shalt have yet, or hit be eve,
> Of every word of thys sentence
> A preve by experience,
> And with thyne eres heren wel
> Top and tayl, and everydel,
> That every word that spoken ys
> Cometh into Fames Hous, ywys,
> As I have seyd; what wilt thou more?"
>
> (875–83)

"All this"—the implication is—"and more—much more": everything, in short, that it is in the lecturer's mind ruthlessly and benevolently to deign to explain. The point is underlined, from the helpless victim's point of view, by yet further "soaring" on the eagle's part, accompanied by a complacent assertion of the strength of its own position:

> "Be seynt Jame,
> Now wil we speken al of game!",
>
> (885–86)

an assertion followed by a solicitous inquiry concerning the welfare of its burden: "'How farest thou?' quod he to me" (887); and the answer, as inevitable as it is finally noncommittal, comes from the poet in the form of another expression of helpless acquiescence: "'Wel,' quod I."

With his situation made clear in this way, the poet is borne upward into the heavens, something after the fashion of Dante following Beatrice upward through the spheres of Paradise, but in a very different mood and to a notably dissimilar destination. Like the Italian poet, his English successor is moved to philosophical considerations in the course of his ascent. Boethius comes into his mind, as well as other authorities in these cosmological matters—"Marcian" and "Anteclaudian" (985–86), for example—but the effect is notably different from that conveyed by Dante's consciously expanding awareness of the amplitude of his theme. Chaucer, like Dante, is moved at one point to question whether he finds himself in body or in spirit[9] and to confess, again like Dante, and like St. Paul whom Dante was echoing[10] that he does not know the answer: "I not, ywys; but God, thou wost" (982). The effect in Chaucer is, however, very noticeably less "heroic" than it had been in Dante, for he confesses himself as without any desire to undertake this dangerous journey, or to arrive at the knowledge to which it may lead him:

> With that this egel gan to crye,
> "Lat be," quod he, "thy fantasye!
> Wilt thou lere of sterres aught?"
>
> (991–93)

Dante's ascent through Paradise is marked by an expanding "thirst" for knowledge and understanding, which grows unquenchably after the manner of true, spiritual experience.[11] It constitutes, for Dante, at once his source of inspiration and his mortal peril; but Chaucer has no wish to follow in these paths and presents himself in a lower, notably more human (and comically self-deprecating) key. His answer to the bird-lecturer's challenge is an unequivocal refusal: "'Nay, certeynly,' quod y, 'ryght naught'" (994). The refusal strikes the eagle as both incomprehensible and inconvenient. "And why?" it inquires, not without a note of impatience, and receives a modest and very human reply: "For y am now to old" (995).

The bird, having embarked upon its exposition, is not so easily deterred from pursuing it. It goes on, scarcely heeding the poet's last words, to offer him a glimpse of the splendors that might have been his, had he cared to accept the offer made to him:

> "Elles I wolde the have told,"
> Quod he, "the sterres names, lo,
> And al the hevenes sygnes therto,
> And which they ben."
>
> (996–99)

Once again there is a reference here to the explanations that Beatrice offers to satisfy Dante's compelling and increasing desire to be informed as they rise together through the successive spheres of Paradise; but Chaucer's response amounts to a notably negative, conscious denial of any wish to know these things. "'No fors,' quod y." Faced by this irritating refusal, which threatens to prevent it from experiencing the satisfaction it has promised to itself as omniscient expositor, the eagle insists on its pedagogical purpose. "Yis, pardee!" it says, and seeks to draw out a further question, "wostow why?" (1000). The argument is that the poet will need the scholarly information it can give in order to read poetry with a proper understanding. How, otherwise, will he be able to appreciate the references that abound in all respectable verse to gods who are "stellified" and to the places that they occupy in the heavens?

These are matters that the poet, in his ignorance, fails to appreciate, even though he often mentions them in his writings:

> For though thou have hem ofte on honde,
> Yet nostow not wher that they stonde.
>
> (1009–10)

The poet, however, fails to be convinced. It is enough for him that he is able to draw in these matters on previous poets, who knew the truth concerning them and on whom he is content to rely as the occasion arises. "No fors," he obstinately repeats, and adds

> hyt is no nede.
> I leve as wel, so God me spede,
> Hem that write of this matere,
> As though I knew her places here.
>
> (1011–14)

Furthermore, it may be that his eyes—unlike those of Dante, whose power to sustain intensities of light grew through his ascent in response to the successive challenges imposed upon it[12]—are humanly weak, lacking in strength to sustain the offered visions:

> they shynen here so bryghte,
> Hyt shulde shenden al my syghte,
> To loke on hem,
>
> (1015–17)

an observation that, as the bird somewhat ruefully recognizes, may well be true. "That may wel be," it allows, and there is a sense of disappointment implied at the opportunity lost for further instruction, the lecture so frustratingly never to be delivered.

Lecture or no, the poet is being borne inexorably to his destination, and this is now declared as the Second Book approaches its conclusion. It is here, as we have been led to expect, that the elusive "tidings" of Love are to be found. What the bird actually affirms, however, is something at once vaster and more confusing. Raising its voice to a level of almost prophetic intensity, it announces the first sight of the House of Fame and asks, rhetorically, "Maistow not heren that I do?" (1024). The poet's reply is once more somewhat noncommittal—"'What?' quod I"—but it is enough to produce the eagle's further response:

> "The grete soun,"
> Quod he, "that rumbleth up and doun
> In Fames Hous, full of tydynges,
> Bothe of feir speche and chidynges,
> And of fals and soth compouned.
> Herke wel; hyt is not rouned.
> Herestow not the grete swogh?"
>
> (1025–31)

Once again the poet's reply, uttered—we should always remember—from his uncomfortable situation in mid-air, is gently submissive. "'Yis, parde!' quod y, 'wel ynogh,'" and then goes on to suggest the element of unheroic terror in his situation as he answers the questions that follow:

> "And what soun is it lyk?" quod hee.
> "Peter! lyk betynge of the see."
> Quod y, "ayen the roches holowe,
> Whan tempest doth the shippes swalowe."
>
> (1033–36)

We have to respond here to a new element in the poetry, one that, without denying the essentially comic force of most of what we have so far read, carries us into another, and finally serious order of consideration. In the House of Fame, Chaucer is to be exposed to new sources of possible poetry, at once richer, more true to life, and more potentially uncomfortable in the questions they raise, than those which would derive from a continued following of the familiar, but more limited love-conventions.

The theme has points of contact with Chaucer's previous poem. The "dream" of the House of Fame occupies something of the position, in relation to the story of Dido and Aeneas, that the knight's history in *The Book of the Duchess* was found to assume in relation to the tale of Seyx and Alcyone. As the book ends the eagle, which now leaves the poet to his own devices, expresses the hope that some good, in the shape of an increased measure of understanding that will (presumably) affect the poetry he writes, will come of the adventure:

> God of heven sende the grace
> Some good to lernen in this place.
>
> (1087–88)

The "good," however, remains obscure in its outlines. The dream sets out, here as in *The Book of the Duchess,* to find a way of reconciling those two troublesomely unmanageable and incompatible terms to which Chaucer is apt to give the names of *authority* and *experience:* life, if we like, as tradition, in the form of literary convention, would have us see it and as it presents itself to a notably unprejudiced poet in its actual conduct. The need for the reconciliation is recognized: but the result, inasmuch as this significantly unfinished poem presents it, is more inconclusive than ever. The "message" that the poem seems finally to convey, if indeed there is one, is consistently undercut by the typically Chaucerian use of irony.

The House of Fame, at the entrance to which the eagle has left the poet, turns out to be an oddly inconsequential structure. It appears to be founded, not securely on "steel," but on a "rock" of ice, firm in appearance but subject to melting; in the poet's puzzled comment it was "a feble fondament" that speaks unfavorably of the wisdom of the builder—

> He ought him lytel glorifye
> That hereon bilt—
>
> (1134–35)

and that offers little prospect that so insecure a project may prove lasting. The House of Fame is very like what could better be called the dwelling-place of Fortune, and as such the reflection of notorious inconstancy and instability.

When the poet-dreamer enters the House, these doubtful impressions are strongly confirmed. His vision is indeed a thing of beauty, with some of the fascination associated with the great manuscript illustrations of the period:

> But natheles al the substance
> I have yit in my remembrance;
> For whi me thoughte, be seynt Gyle!
> Al was ston of beryle,
> Bothe the castel and the tour,
> And eke the halle and every bour,
> Wythouten peces or joynynges.
> But many subtil compassinges,
> Babewynnes and pynacles,
> Ymageries and tabernacles,
> I say; and ful eke of wyndowes,
> As flakes falle in grete snowes.
> And eke in ech of the pynacles
> Weren sondry habitacles,
> In which stoden, al withoute—
> Ful the castel, al aboute—
> Of all maner of mynstralles,
> And gestiours, that tellen tales
> Both of wepinge and of game,
> Of al that longeth unto Fame.
>
> (1181–1200)

Even here, however, and running through the long description that follows, there is an insistent note of deception, or at least of baseless fantasy, which answers to the dream-state and which is carried on into the picture of the "goddess" Fame to which it leads. The most apparent feature of this deity is an infinite variety: she presents herself alternately as so small

> That the lengthe of a cubite
> Was lengere than she semed be,
>
> (1370–71)

and—a moment later—so "miraculously" grown in dimension

> That with her fet she erthe reighte,
> And with hir hed she touched hevene.
>
> (1374–75)

The effect, appropriate to the dream experience, is to stress the element of "seeming," and so of "illusion." Fame presents herself differently at different times and to separate visions. She offers to her devotees what they wish to find in her, and what they believe—but only believe—they see in her rests finally on their will to see. Of all sizes, a compound of the beautiful and the grotesque, she is saluted as a goddess by those who sing her praises in her dwelling-place:

> And ever mo, eternally,
> They songe of Fame, as thoo herd y:
> "Heryed be thou and thy name,
> Goddesse of Renoun or of Fame!"
>
> (1403–6)

Much in this way may the angelic hosts be thought of as uttering the praises of their Creator; but the question to be asked is, of course, whether such worship can properly be given to a "deity" whose operations are by definition fickle and deceptive.

Much the same impression emerges from the description of the images of the famous dead, set up on pillars round this central presence (1419–1512). One of the pillars, made of iron, is

> peynted, al endelong,
> With tigres blod in every place.
>
> (1458–59)

This is the pillar of the poet Statius, and among the names graven upon it as the theme of his writing is that of "cruel Achilles."[13] Other pillars are given to the writers who dealt with the matter of Troy, and among these there seemed to be "a litel envye," for one of them accuses Homer of distorting the truth—he "made lyes" (1477)—by favoring the Greeks against Troy and so fostering a *false* Fame, based only upon "fable."

The general result, as it appears to the poet, is to produce the sense of "a ful confus matere," in which no kind of solid certainty is available. The long passage that follows (1513–1867) confirms these impressions. The suitors of Fame are heralded by an outburst of sound—"I herde a noyse aprochen blyve,"

> That ferde as been don in an hive
> Ayen her tyme of out-fleynge.
>
> (1522–23)

In what follows we are shown the way in which the favors of Fame, like those of "her suster, dame Fortune," are capriciously granted. The poet is unable to see any reason in what takes place under his eyes. Fame, it seems, refuses her gifts for no reason at all. When her suitors complain, the only answer they get is "For me lyst hyt noght" (1564). She has at her disposal two heralds ("clariouns") named respectively "Laude," or Praise, and "Slander." These operate "in every toune," and sound indifferently, without reference to any true merit or demerit. In all this, Chaucer is developing, after his own fashion, Boethius's conclusions in respect of the fickle "goddess" and the attitude that wise men will adopt toward her.[14] Happiness consists in looking beyond the turning of Fortune's wheel, in receiving her "gifts" with indifference, recognizing that it is in their nature not to last. The truly wise man will place his confidence in the stable Providence that lies beyond these meaningless vicissitudes.

At this point, however, and in the real world available to poets as to the rest of men, the vicissitudes prevail, to the apparent exclusion of all rationality and even common sense. The good works of the virtuous fail to achieve the fame that it seems should by reason be theirs:

> Y graunte yow
> That ye shal have a shrewed fame,
> And wikkyd loos, and worse name,
> Though ye good loos have wel deserved.
>
> (1618–21)

This does not prevent others, apparently indistinguishable, from having their petitions granted. Again, some of those who from modesty express the desire to have the fame of their good deeds concealed are given their wish; but another group, who made the same request, find that the works that they, as "contemplatives," wished to keep hidden are published to the world. Those who in their lives achieved nothing, either in deeds or in love, ask to be renowned like their opposites. Their desire is granted; but yet another group, who have the same request to make, find it rejected and themselves the object of ridicule. The wicked too—the "shrews"—ask to be made famous for their perverse behavior. Since such men as he who burned "the temple of Ysidis" (1844) in Athens cannot receive praise for good works, let them be remembered for the evil they have accomplished. This petition turns out to be granted.

It is hard not to feel through all this that Chaucer is offering comment, in his own deliberately disingenuous way, on the insistence of other poets—and most notably his great Italian predecessors, Dante and Petrarch—upon the achievement of fame as a spur to their creation. At all events, when he has come to the end of his catalogue of misplaced and obscurely answered aspirations, he expressly disclaims for himself any desire to obtain the favors of this equivocal power:

> With that y gan aboute wende,
> For oon that stood ryght at my bak,
> Me thoughte, goodly to me spak,

> And seyde, "Frend, what is thy name?
> Artow come hider to han fame?"
> "Nay, for sothe, frend," quod y;
> "I cam noght hyder, graunt mercy,
> For no such cause, by my hed!
> Sufficeth me, as I were ded,
> That no wight have my name in honde.
> I wot myself best how y stonde;
> For what I drye, or what I thynke,
> I wil myselven al hyt drynke,
> Certeyn, for the more part,
> As fer forth as I kan myn art."
>
> (1868–82)

The affirmation stands out with a certain seriousness of emphasis against the comic sense of much that has gone before. Chaucer seems to be saying that he proposes to set aside the literary objectives that have moved other poets and that he sees as leading only to likely deception. He sees himself as engaged in an effort to understand the true potentialities of his art and to work them out in the conscious development of his craft. "I wot myself best how y stonde": there is a significant note of self-reliance, even of proper pride, in this assertion, which is compatible with the equally proper humility of an artist who is conscious of the serious tasks ahead and engaged in trying to see how, given his own situation and gifts, these tasks may best be approached to arrive at the goal of valid and personally fulfilling creation.

In the lines that follow the poet confronts his situation with a remarkable honesty. He has come to this strange place in the expectation of "tidings" that will illuminate for him the true nature of the "love" that it seems that poets are destined so indefatigably and so uncertainly to pursue. The "tidings" were, in his expectation, to be *new*, revelatory; but he has to confess that he came without knowing, in reality, just what to expect:

> "But what doost thou here than?" quod he.
> Quod y, "That wyl y tellen the,
> The cause why y stonde here:
> Somme newe tydynges for to lere,
> Somme newe thinges, y not what,
> Tydynges, other this or that,
> Of love, or suche thynges glade."
>
> (1883–89)

The implication seems to be that the poet came with a sense, or an expectation, that the old "love" theme would in some way be renewed, rendered a source of new inspiration. The reality has proved to be a deep disappointment, the apparent reversal of all the certainties that, he had been led to expect, would constitute a source of continuing life for his art. Instead of the expected revelation, he has found, disquietingly and confusingly, just—*nothing*:

> For certeynly, he that me made
> To comen hyder, seyde me,
> Y shulde bothe here and se,
> In this place, wonder thynges;
> But these be no suche tydynges
> As I mene of." "Noo?" quod he.
> And I answered, "Noo, parde!"
>
> (1890–96)

Literary tradition, upon which the poet placed his reliance, has led him, it seems, only to confusion. Love is not, in its truth, what those who formed the convention made it out to be. The reality is not a neatly defined picture, such as previous poets (including some very great ones) have proposed, but a bundle of particular incongruities, a mixture of fulfillments, disappointments, and absurdities through which a poet—like any other man—has to make his way as best he can.

At this point, it seems, the real sense of the whole dream episode begins to emerge, and with it Chaucer's purpose in writing this elusive and tentative poem: elusive and tentative because it answers in all honesty to the present exploratory state of the poet's imagining. The dreamer has discovered that the "tidings" of which he is in search are simply not to be found where he had been led to expect that they were laid up. The search has to be continued elsewhere, in relation to other and less neatly defined conceptions both of life and of poetry. It is at this moment that a messenger arrives to take him from the House of Fame to another place—one, as it turns out, even more confusing, but for that reason more lively—in which he may hope at least to glimpse the solution of his dilemma.

The new place is called *Laboryntus,* or *Domus Dedaly* (1920–21): a place that has not even the appearance of permanence offered by the House of Fame, but that is more fundamentally shifting and evanescent:

> And ever mo, as swyft as thought,
> This queynte hous aboute wente,
> That never mo hyt stille stente.
>
> (1924–26)

The following description, given at considerable length (1927–85), confirms the nature of the place as a "dream-fantasy," a product of human thought working upon the contradictions and obscurities that a dispassionate consideration of our experience is likely to reveal. The house itself evades all rational description. It appeared to the dreamer as "sixty myle of lengthe" (1979); it was made entirely of insubstantial "twigs," and was in perpetual motion. Everything about it is contradictory, nothing concordant. What comes out of it is an endless babel of confused sound, answering to the appetites and aspirations that move men and express themselves in a welter of apparently meaningless activity:

> And be day, in every tyde,
> Been al the dores opened wide,
> And by nyght, echon, unshette;
> Ne porter ther is noon to lette
> No maner tydynges in to pace.
> Ne never rest is in that place
> That hit nys fild ful of tydynges,
> Other loude, or of whisprynges.
>
> (1951–58)

The poet, who has come in search of "tidings," secure orientations in respect of his craft, finds himself confronted with a multiplicity of impressions, all contradictory and confusing, and all—it seems—quite beyond the possibility of reducing them to some kind of artistic order.

The sound that proceeds from this strange mansion is a compound of all the unresolved disorders that constitute man's normal life on earth:

> And over alle the houses angles
> Ys ful of rounynges and of jangles
> Of werres, of pes, of mariages,
> Of reste, of labour, of viages,
> Of abood, of deeth, of lyf,
> Of love, of hate, acord, of stryf,
> Of loos, of lore, and of wynnynges,
> Of hele, of seknesse, of bildynges,
> Of faire wyndes, and of tempestes,
> Of qwalm of folk, and eke of bestes;
> Of dyvers transmutacions
> Of estats, and eke of regions;
> Of trust, of drede, of jelousye,
> Of wit, of wynnynge, of folye;
> Of plente, and of gret famyne,
> Of chepe, of derthe, and of ruyne;
> Of good or mys governement,
> Of fyr, and of dyvers accident.
>
> (1959–76)

Such, it seems, received in no order and apparently susceptible to none, is the material that real life, as distinct from its tidy reflection in literary convention, offers the poet. It is this life, he now knows, that he has somehow to reflect, and in the process of reflecting it to bring to an order that will answer to the nature of reality. The solution to his problem lies at this stage certainly outside the poet's capacity. Indeed, it could be said that Chaucer's mature work is a series of attempts to resolve it, none of them final—for finality is beyond the reach of men in their time-conditioned existence—but each answering to a further step in his understanding of the possibilities of his art and its relationship to the tradition that constituted his original point of departure.

All this time the eagle has been waiting outside. To it the dreamer now turns, asking for permission to enter the Labyrinth in the hope that

> y may lere
> Som good thereon, or sumwhat here
> That leef me were, or that y wente.
>
> (1997–99)

What he hopes to find, no doubt, is "tidings of love" that may answer to his growing sense of his own poetry. The eagle, acceding to this request, affirms that this is precisely the reason why he has been brought to this place. It also stresses that he will still need its guidance to avoid the confusion and despair that he is likely to encounter. Here again, and more especially in the bird's assertion that these trials *have* a purpose, that they answer to what "Jove" of his "grace" has willed with the intention of bringing the dreamer finally to "solace" (2007–9), we may find the real sense of this strange story emerging.

The Labyrinth, when the dreamer at last enters it, is full of the bearers of "Rumour," whose broken exchanges are vividly conveyed:

> And every wight that I saugh there
> Rouned everych in others ere
> A newe tydynge prively,
> Or elles tolde al openly
> Ryght thus, and seyde: "Nost not thou
> That ys betyd, lo, late or now?"
> "No," quod he, "telle me what."
> And than he tolde hym this and that,
> And swor therto that hit was soth—
> "Thus hath he sayd," and "Thus he doth,"
> "Thus shal hit be," "Thus herde y seye,"
> "That shal be founde," "That dar I leye."
>
> (2043–54)

The House of Fame

It is significant, and indicative of a poet who is feeling his way to the expression of his true genius, that the lines warm to a growing sense of the incalculable, even the contradictory nature of human experiences as they are recreated—and deformed in the process—by passing from mouth to mouth. The deforming nature of the process is vividly conveyed, as is the inextricable binding together of mingled truth and falsehood, each striving to assert its priority against the other:

> And somtyme saugh I thoo at ones
> A lesyng and a sad soth sawe
> That gonne of aventure drawe
> Out at a wyndowe for to pace;
> And, when they metten in that place,
> They were achekked bothe two,
> And neyther of hem moste out goo
> For other, so they gonne crowde,
> Til ech of hem gan crien lowde,
> "Lat me go first!" "Nay, but let me!
> And here I wol ensuren the
> Wyth the nones that thou wolt do so,
> That I shal never fro the go,
> But be thyn owne sworen brother!
> We wil medle us ech with other,
> That no man, be they never so wrothe,
> Shal han on of us two, but bothe
> At ones, al besyde his leve,
> Come we a-morwe or on eve,
> Be we cried or stille yrouned."
> Thus saugh I fals and soth compouned
> Togeder fle for oo tydynge.
>
> (2088–2109)

This sense of the comic incongruity of things is already very close to the mode of Chaucer's genius. Perhaps the ultimate sense of this necessarily inconclusive poem lies in bringing this intuition of things to the light and in underlining the inadequacy of the traditional modes upon which his poetry has so far relied to correspond to the real sense of what his experience now prompts him to say.

As the poem draws toward a close that, perhaps significantly, is never made explicit, this sense of the incongruous assumes an increasingly human form. The poet is surrounded in his dream by the rumor-mongers whom, no doubt, he has had ample occasion to observe in his waking life without the intervention of any bird-messenger. All are engaged, with an increasing frenzy that seems to herald the approach of some decisive revelation, in seeking to give, and at the same time to receive, new and contradictory "tidings":

> And, Lord, this hous in alle tymes,
> Was ful of shipmen and pilgrimes,
> With scrippes bret-ful of lesinges,
> Entremedled with tydynges,
> And eek allone be hemselve.
> O, many a thousand tymes twelve
> Saugh I eke of these pardoners,
> Currours, and eke messagers,
> With boystes crammed ful of lyes
> As ever vessel was with lyes.
>
> (2121–30)

It is not an accident, perhaps, that there are moments here—the references to "pilgrims" and "pardoners," to scripts "bret-ful of lesinges" (flatterings), to "tidings" of many contrasts, with truth and lies inseparably joined—that come to us with premonitions that seem to be confirmed in *The Canterbury Tales*. It is as though Chaucer were feeling his way to separate himself from assumptions concerning his art that he was coming to find inadequate, and declaring his intention to offer a reflection of "reality" that should answer to his sense of the infinite unexpectedness of life, its refusal to be molded into narrow conventional limits, and its insistent demand to be given fully "comic"—but not on that account less serious—expression.

At the last, however, the dreamer returns, however belatedly, to his original search for "love-tidings." That, we remember, was his purpose as he embarked upon his poem; but it is a purpose that has been in great measure overtaken by what he has seen in his exploration of the "Labyrinth." Moved by the pressure of those around him, he feels himself making his way to—he does not quite know what, but in any case toward an object of universal attraction:

> I herde a gret noyse withalle
> In a corner of the halle,
> Ther men of love-tydynges tolde,
> And I gan thiderward beholde;
> For I saugh rennynge every wight,
> As faste as that they hadden myght;
> And everych cried, "What thing is that?"
> And somme seyde, "I not never what."
>
> (2141–48)

The general impression is less one of an approaching revelation than of continuing confusion, expressed, however, with an equal sense of encompassing if disordered, living energy. It seems that there was to have been, to end the poem, a kind of "revelation" or clarification; but the poem breaks off abruptly before we can learn in what it consisted. Mention is made, in the last line of all, to the appearance of "a man of gret auctorite" (2158); a man, presumably, who would announce the "tidings" of which the dreamer has been in search. But what exactly these tidings were to have been remains unspecified. If Chaucer were still at this point following traditional conceptions of love, as laid down by other poets, we might have been told that "love"—like all the varied human concerns that have been presented through the image of the "Labyrinth"—contains a large element of delusion, and that the only valid "love" is that which—in a view that we might call "Boethian"—transcends time and circumstance inasmuch as it is related to *Caritas*. If that was to be the lesson, however, it is one that would seem, if not to contradict, at least to read strangely in relation to the comic matter that has dominated the later parts of the poem.

Chaucer, perhaps, is likely to have felt that such a conclusion would be inartistic, and indeed insufficient as a resolution of the poem he had actually written, a poem that tends to a different and distinct approach to life, and one that he was not yet ready to develop in its fullness. The poem remains, perhaps of set purpose, open-ended, unfinished; it may well be that its only fitting continuation was to be the writing, in due course, of another and greater work, in which human life should be explored under the guise of pilgrimage and in which its intractable individuality, the sense of different motives and different levels of awareness of these motives, should be seen as tending indeed toward an end, but one that is not, in time and on earth, likely to be realized in its totality.

4
The Parliament of Fowls

The third of Chaucer's earliest poems—*The Parliament of Fowls*—may strike us as a more finished performance than *The House of Fame*. The poem seems to present itself with a clearer purpose, not to be—at least formally speaking—inconclusive in the way so apparent in its predecessor. Chaucer has also, we may feel, gained by having come to understand the limitations of the octosyllabic line he used in the two earlier poems. Here he has moved to a more ample decasyllabic line and developed, to go with it, a seven-line stanza, the model for which he found in the French measure known as *rime roial*. These novelties coexist in the poem with other elements, more traditional and "English" in their effect. To take the most obvious instance, the idea of a debate between birds, who reflect some of the characteristics of human beings, had already in the thirteenth century produced *The Owl and the Nightingale*,[1] a poem of surprising—and, it could be argued, premature—originality.

The *Parliament* opens with an introduction covering four stanzas, which we have already considered in relation to the development of Chaucer's poetics and prosody.[2] In it, the poet speaks of the difficulties he has encountered in the pursuit of love, but does so in terms that underline the close connection between the lover's condition and the exercise of his craft. The two themes of "love" and poetry are seen as different aspects of a single reality. "Love" is the proper, indeed the natural subject of poetry, and by discussing it in terms of his art the poet finds himself raising questions that are central and vital to human life. He presents himself in a state of disorientation in his relation to this powerful and disturbing aspect of his creativity, though it must be emphasized that it would be rash to read these declarations as conveying any meaning of a directly "autobiographical" kind. What we are given is the use of convention for ends that transcend the personal and that have to do with the writing of verse but that look beyond this to more universal attributes of life.

Chaucer, however, having suggested these aspects of his theme, characteristically distances himself from them, expressly denying that he—or the *persona* he has created in his image—has any direct knowledge of the theme he has chosen:

> For al be that I knowe nat Love in dede,
> Ne wot how that he quiteth folk here hyre.
>
> (8–9)

He insists that such knowledge as he has is derived from his book-reading, in other words from the "authority" whose relation to "experience" has so often concerned him. This source of understanding is sufficient to bring home to him the essentially ambivalent nature of this power as a compound of "myrakles" and "crewel yre" (11). What is certain is that Love will be "lord and syre" (12), a dominating force in the life of men; but to what ends he wields his power—his "strokes" that are "so sore"—is very much an open question.

The next two stanzas, concluding the introduction, carry these meditations further. The poet tells us that he was, after his usual custom, reading a book that "was write with lettres olde" (19), that had the prestige attached to venerable tradition. This, as he also points out, has long been a custom of his: "On bokes rede I ofte, as I yow tolde" (16); we may perhaps think that this habit is at once his strength and his limitation. He was, he next tells us, reading with a purpose in view, "a certeyn thing to lerne" (20): a "thing" no doubt connected with his constant desire to understand the nature of the "love" that, again following custom and tradition, he has taken to be the proper theme of poetry. The question that now presents itself has already been indicated: is this "love" a beneficient, life-giving force, an affirmation of human creativity, or is it rather a deception, a source of suffering and disillusionment? There is much "authority" to be found for either of these views in the books that the poet has for so long and so obsessively consulted.

Initially, the poet is ready to believe that his reading can give him the answer he needs to his questions. The introduction ends on an affirmation of the relevance of literary tradition as a source of true understanding:

> For out of old feldes, as men seyth,
> Cometh al this newe corn from yer to yere,

And out of olde bokes, in good feyth,
Cometh al this newe science that men lere.

(22–25)

The lines amount to an impressive statement of the valid part played by tradition in promoting understanding in the present. "Old books" are the repositories, handed down through successive generations, of the wisdom acquired through past experience. Its purpose, however, inasmuch as it is true and living tradition and something more than a container of dead ideas and attitudes, is to produce *new* fruit in the present. "New corn" springs up "from year to year" in "old fields," and it is the newness, the continuing process of rebirth, that finally matters. The only kind of tradition that can justify the poet's continued poring upon the texts of the past, which he says has filled him with so much delight "That al that day me thoughte but a lyte" (28) is that which is capable of renewing itself, of being continually put to test by reference to the needs of the present. Up to a point the poem to follow is a probing of this notion through exposure to the successive stages of a process of "experience." The notion has come to him through "authority," as something that "men seyeth." It needs to be confirmed, rendered actual, in its relation to the real "experience" of an individual poet.

The book upon which Chaucer turns out to have been concentrating is one of the most influential works that brought the doctrine of classical antiquity to the attention of the Middle Ages. It is a version of Cicero's *Dream of Scipio (Somnium Scipionis)*,[3] with the commentary, written round A.D. 400 by Macrobius. Written at a time when the original texts were still available, the interest of the work for subsequent ages lay in the reading of its "pagan" matter in a Christian key, which made it acceptable to the new age. In Cicero's original version the younger Scipio, after speaking of his father, Africanus, to the King of Numidia, has a dream in which the dead man appears to him and discourses on the afterlife. It was the thought on this subject expressed by a great writer of classical times— a man of "authority" indeed—that accounts for the interest of subsequent generations in the work and for its influence upon some of the greatest writers of the Christian Middle Ages.

The dream itself does not seem on a first reading to have much bearing on the subject of "love" as announced in the introductory stanzas. In it Africanus shows his son Carthage, the scene of his great victory for Rome, from the point of vantage of a "starry place": we are reminded of Dante's ascent to the *Primum Mobile* in the *Paradiso* and of his downward glance at the earth he has left behind,[4] as well as—by anticipation—of Troilus's similar assumption into the spheres after his death at the hands of the "fierse Achille."[5] Scipio is also shown in the dream that those who dedicate their lives to the common good—"comune profyt"⁶—are rewarded by the gift of eternal life:

> (They) shulde into a blysful place wende,
> There as joye is that last withouten ende.
>
> (48–49)

Life on earth is seen in terms of the dream as "but a maner deth" (54), from which release comes in heaven. A comparison is drawn between the insignificance of the terrestrial globe and the splendor of the celestial spheres and the harmonies of heaven:

> Thanne shewede he hym the lytel erthe that here is,
> At regard of the hevenes quantite;
> And after shewede he hym the nyne speres,
> And after that the melodye herde he
> That cometh of thilke speres thryes thre,
> That welle is of musik and melodye
> In this world here, and cause of armonye.
>
> Than bad he hym, syn erthe was so lyte,
> And ful of torment and of harde grace,
> That he ne shulde hym in the world delyte.
> Thanne tolde he hym, in certeyn yeres space
> That every sterre shulde come into his place
> Ther it was first, and al shulde out of mynde
> That in this world is don of al mankynde.
>
> (57–70)

The lesson drawn by Scipio from this vision, and enjoined upon him by Africanus as a message for all men, is given in his own words:

> Know thyself first immortal,
> And loke ay besyly thow werche and wysse
> To commune profit, and thow shalt not mysse
> To comen swiftly to that place deere
> That ful of blysse is and of soules cleere.
>
> (73–77)

The wicked, on the contrary, will undergo a kind of purgatorial process, until "foryeven al hir wikked dede,"

> Than shul they come into this blysful place,
> To which to comen God the sende his grace.
>
> (83–84)

It should be noted that, although this is a pagan's dream, and though the final destiny of the impenitent is not the eternal self-exclusion proposed by orthodox Christian teaching, the reference to "grace" and "heaven" carry a specifically Christian content.

At the end of the dream, the poet is left in a state of some dissatisfaction. He has received a "lesson" from authority, but it has left him in notable puzzlement; for he has not been granted what he was looking for—"tidings of love"—and what he has been given is not what he thinks he wants:

> For bothe I hadde thyng which that I nolde,
> And ek I nadde that thyng that I wolde.
>
> (90–91)

In its essence this is the very situation that induced the poet to leave *The House of Fame* unfinished. It is possible that the tidings to be announced by the "man of great authority" may have been intended to be not unlike those now offered to the poet through Scipio's vision. Perhaps there too the lesson would have been one of otherworldliness, of a love that is justified in the measure in which it is able to look beyond the temporal and see itself in relation to the eternal creative purposes of the universe. If this is so, in both poems the "answer" offered to his problem leaves the poet notably uncommitted. What he has asked for is "tidings" of love; what he has been given is something essentially different, which can hardly be reconciled either to the kind of poetry he has so far written, or that which he would wish to write. What he has learned in his vision is no doubt true, and important, but it does not answer to his immediate needs. His creative purposes still have to find a suitable form of expression, which can be neither that of the conventional love poets nor that of the otherworldly moralists. The form adequate to his purposes is one that still has to be found; the rest of *The Parliament of Fowls* will be another inconclusive attempt to find it.

Tired of his exertions, Chaucer describes himself as retiring to bed after his reading (92–94) and as dreaming that Africanus appears to him to offer a reward for the patience he has shown in going through Macrobius's "olde boke." The dream, which is to constitute the main body of the poem, begins with a vision of the Garden of Love, a vision strangely and deliberately ambivalent, and which aims at presenting the two faces of love: the faces respectively, let us say, of life and death contained in it. The invocation is to Cytherea—Venus, the goddess of blind passion—and to her son Cupid. The help she may be expected to give is likely to be at least as much deceptive as real: that is what seems to be suggested in the phrase "As wisly as I sey the north-north-west" (117),[7] which the poet artlessly introduces at this point.

As soon as this equivocal invocation is completed we are placed, in the poet's dream, before the gate leading into the Garden. The gate bears an inscription, "with lettres large iwroughte," which carries a definite reminiscence of the words that appeared on the gateway to Dante's *Inferno*.[8] Here, however, there are two inscriptions, where Dante has one, and they stand in substantial contradiction to one another. The first offers strong intimations of fulfilment to be obtained through love:

> Thorgh me men gon into that blysful place
> Of hertes hele and dedly woundes cure;
> Thorgh me men gon unto the welle of grace,
> There grene and lusty May shal evere endure.
> This is the wey to al good adventure.
> Be glad, thow redere, and thy sorwe of-caste;
> Al open am I—passe in, and sped thee faste!
>
> (127–33)

The invitation is to enter a place of happiness, where the life of springtime ("grene and lusty May") offers itself in terms of the supernatural fulfillment of "grace." The equation of the two orders is, we may think, both attractive and overly facile. The very fact that this gate declares itself to be "all open," inviting the traveler to "passe in, and sped thee faste," carries a suggestion that what is offered may represent rather a nostalgic wish than a reality, that true happiness—"al good aventure"—is not to be had by trusting simply and blindly to chance, to the ambiguous operations of Fortune. This would certainly be in accordance with the teachings of respectable "authority." Whether, or to what extent, it can be found to answer to a poet's individual experience is a question that will continue to concern Chaucer in all his work.

However this may be, side by side with the first inscription, there is another, of very different aspect, menacing and dark in content:

> "Thorgh me men gon," then spak that other side,
> "Unto the mortal strokes of the spere
> Of which Disdayn and Daunger is the gyde,
> Ther nevere tre shal fruyt ne leves bere.
> This strem yow ledeth to the sorweful were
> There as the fish in prysoun is al drye;
> Th'eschewing is only the remedye!"
>
> (134–40)

Where the first gate offered life, or the appearance of it, the second seems to convey threatening associations of death. It bears a warning to escape the perils, the *Disdayne* and *Daunger*[9] that constitute the less enticing face of love and that only the "eschewing" of its enticements can avoid.

Faced by these contrary prospects, the poet is unable to make his choice between entering and turning away, until Africanus overcomes his hesitation by the simple expedient of pushing him through the entrance—"Me hente, and shof in at the gates wide" (154)—pointing out that, since he has confessed that he is not "Loves servaunt," he can be in no danger from the god's operations:

> For thow of love hast lost thy tast, I gesse,
> As sek man hath of swete and bytternesse.
>
> (160–61)

Himself unable to love, the poet can perhaps learn something about the nature of that passion by observing the results of its operations in others:

> although that thow be dul,
> Yit that thow canst not do, yit mayst thow se.
>
> (162–63)

A man, Africanus argues, may be incapable of undergoing the challenge of wrestling (he "may not stonde a pul") and yet be a witness at the contest. If—to revert to his own concern as a poet—he has the necessary skill in his craft—"connying for t'endite" (167)—he will be given "mater of to wryte." What the disoriented narrator seems to be invited to explore in his dream is, not simply the truth or falsity of various current notions of "love," but the relation of lived experience to the creative process. Chaucer may present himself as less than adequate as a "lover" in the terms that literary convention has established and that have found issue in a kind of poetry that he has come to find unsatisfactory; but he may yet be able to contemplate the actual behavior of those subjected to this—or, indeed, to any other force of life—and to turn the results of his reflection into poetic creation.

The Garden of Love, into which the poet-dreamer now enters, is a typically ambivalent Chaucerian conception. In its first projection it recalls the Garden of Eden, as it might have been before the Fall: a place of innocence, untouched by awareness of good and evil. In this innocence lies its attraction and its fatal weakness. The sight of the trees fills the newcomer with joy; as he says, "But, Lord, so I was glad and wel begoon!":

> For overal where that I myne eyen caste
> Were trees clad with leves that ay shal laste,
> Ech in his kynde, of colour fresh and greene
> As emeraude, that joye was to seene.
>
> (172–75)

There follows the description of the various aspects of the garden—the flowers, the river, and the fishes—as the newly entered dreamer comes upon them; finally, of the birds and beasts that fill it with joyous music:

> On every bow the bryddes herde I synge,
> With voys of aungel in here armonye;
> Some besyede hem here bryddes forth to brynge;
> The litel conyes to here pley gonne hye;
> And ferther al aboute I gan espye
> The dredful ro, the buk, the hert and hynde,
> Squyrels, and bestes smale of gentil kynde.
>
> Of instruments of strenges in acord
> Herde I so pleye a ravyshyng swetnesse,
> That God, that makere is of al and lord,
> Ne herde nevere beter, as I gesse.
> Therwith a wynd, unnethe it myghte be lesse,
> Made in the leves grene a noyse softe
> Accordaunt to the foules song alofte.
>
> Th'air of that place so attempre was
> That nevere was ther grevuance of hot ne cold;
> There wex ek every holsom spice and gras;
> No man may there waxe sek ne old;
> Yit was there joye more a thousandfold
> Than man can telle; ne nevere wolde it nyghte,
> But ay cler day to any manes syghte.
>
> (190–210)

The description reminds us of the moment in which Dante, near the summit of the Mount of Purgatory, enters the Earthly Paradise and meets its mysterious guardian in the person of Matelda.[10] Like Dante's setting it is less a natural place than a human aspiration, a reflection of man's desire to see his environment as reflecting the order, the harmony, and the state of timeless abstraction from mutability and death to which intensely, and in time vainly, he yearns. The Garden has come into being through the operations of Love under its more benign, but at least partially illusory aspect. It answers to an innate human desire that life should be lived in abstraction from the pressure of time-conditioned reality, at once more beautiful and less real than the world as it has presented itself to all men since the decisive reality of the Fall.

Already, however, there are signs that the inhabitants of the Garden, variously dedicated to the fulfillments of Love, exhibit a considerable degree of ambivalence. Under a tree the dreamer comes upon "Cupide, oure lord" (but is he, we may ask, our rightful "lord"?) and "Wille, his doughter," who is closely connected, in a way scarcely compatible with the changeless, nontemporal quality so powerfully present in the Garden, with the restless compulsions of sensual desire.[11] Between them, Cupid and Will are preparing to shoot their arrows, arrows that, far from serving the ends of life, can serve "Some for to sle, and some to wounde and kerve" (217). The farther we penetrate into the Garden, the more we see that the various personifications that inhabit it answer at least as much to death as to life. Some of them can be considered positive, life-enhancing; but even about most of these there is an air of ambivalence, and others bear connotations of scarcely disguised menace and stress:

> Tho was I war of Plesaunce anon-ryght,
> And of Aray, and Lust, and Curteysie,
> And of the Craft that can and hath the myght
> To don by force a wyght to don folye—
> Disfigurat was she, I nyl nat lye.
>
> (218–22)

The greater part of these attributes are as much dedicated to ends of deception and disappointment as to those of serenity and fulfillment. The women who dance about the Temple of Love are, like maenads, "al dishevele" (235), disarrayed; and the "doves" that flutter round them are as much connected with unbridled sensuality as with peace and lasting happiness.

The sounds to be heard from the Temple, moreover, are not those of happy fulfillment. They are sighs, expressive above all of the pains of jealousy:

> Withinne the temple, of sykes hoote as fyr
> I herde a swogh that gan aboute renne,
> Whiche sikes were engendered with desyr,
> That maden every auter for to brenne
> Of newe flaume, and wel espyed I thenne
> That al the cause of sorwes that they drye
> Cam of the bittere goddesse Jelousye.
>
> (246–52)

Possessiveness and unchecked self-assertion are signs of *false* love; but, as the dreamer sees them, they are inseparable from the following of Venus.[12] Priapus, too, who stands "in sovereyn place" (254) in the Temple, is the most ambivalent of deities.[13] He is, on the one hand, the god of gardens and of distinctively human, civilized cultivation, but he is also the god of sensual desire, so that it is appropriate that his worship—

> In swych aray as whan the asse hym shente
> With cri by nyghte, and with hys sceptre in honde—
>
> (255–56)

should be a double-edged affair, largely compounded with absurdity and excess. Venus herself occupies "a prive corner" (260), a dark place in the temple. She is "naked from the brest unto the hed" (269), sensually enticing but deceptive; and she is surrounded by decidedly equivocal powers—by Bacchus, god of wine, a deity dedicated, if we will, to life, but also to drunken excess, and, less ambiguously in her life-giving significance, by Ceres, goddess of the harvest. At her feet are two "yonge folk" (278), praying (they "cride") to the "Cyprian" for help in their love concerns. Diana, goddess of chastity, is also evoked, but in negative terms, for the temple walls are hung with many a broken bow

> Of maydenes swich as gonne here tymes waste
> In hyre servyse;
>
> (283–84)

and the walls are painted with examples of unhappiness in the pursuit of passion:

> Alle these were peynted on that other syde,
> And al here love, and in what plyt they dyde.
>
> (293–94)

Evidently, devotion to "Venus," universal as it is, set inescapably at the heart of the Garden, is at least as much a source of disappointment and death as of the fulfillment that it seems, so enticingly and so deceptively, to offer.

As though in search of relief from these obscurities the dreamer returns to the Garden and the daylight world. He finds there the enthroned figure of Nature, surrounded by the fowls of the air gathered to choose their mates on the day dedicated to St. Valentine. This vision of "the noble goddesse Nature" (303) opens a new and, as the poet seems to hope, a more positive stage in the poem. As much is suggested by the lines that introduce the new apparition:

> Whan I was come ayeyn into the place
> That I of spak, that was so sote and grene,
> Forth welk I tho myselven to solace.
> Tho was I war wher that sat a queene
> That, as of lyght the somer sonne shene
> Passeth the sterre, right so over mesure
> She fayrer was than any creature.
>
> (295–301)

The surprising beauty of the new vision is stressed in a way that indicates a contrast with the preceding figure of Venus. Nature is connected with the love that fulfills itself by bringing new life into being, and that finds its proper consummation in the marriages that she will ratify by her presence. Venus, on the other hand, is the goddess of "desire," which can be creative when it operates within the framework set by Nature as the superior deity, the handmaid of the Creator's loving purpose, but which can readily turn, out of this context, into a force essentially egoistic and acquisitive, seeking the isolated assertion of the self and ending, for that very reason, in disappointment and, in the extreme case, in death.

At the end of his dream tour of the Garden, then, the poet has introduced the goddess "Nature" and set her up in contrast to the figure of Venus. To grasp the full implications of this contrast, which is important both for the poem and for an understanding of Chaucer's thought in general, it is necessary to go some way back in time to search for certain concepts of central concern to medieval thinking on the subject of love. Generally speaking, Christian thought between the years 400 and 1000 tended to see the world in terms of a contrast between an eternally stable order of the spirit and a corrupt, or deceptive temporal reality. The proper end of human life was conceived as lying beyond the vicissitudes of the worlds of time, in which sin and its consequence, death, prevailed. At about the year 1000, however, reflecting no doubt expanding social conditions and the more tolerable and more ordered state of material life that they brought with them, less extreme currents of thought made their influence felt. They are largely associated with a tradition, derived ultimately from Plato, largely lost in the West during the intervening centuries, but kept alive through the work of such men as Macrobius and Boethius. During the later Middle Ages only one Platonic dialogue—the *Timaeus*—was directly known, and then only in incomplete translation.[14] The available fragment contained, however, Plato's myth of creation and this, in a Christianized form, exercised a powerful influence upon medieval ways of thinking.

As interpreted in the light of Christian doctrine, the *Timaeus* posed certain questions about the nature of the universe that were of great concern to medieval thinkers. Plato had held that the "real" world was the eternal realm of the Ideas, of which everyday "reality" was, at best, a pale and imperfect reflection. The world of Ideas is the world of Being, the world that really *is*. Such a notion was evidently likely to attract a transcendentally oriented faith; but it raised in a very direct form questions of notably difficult resolution. Given the supreme reality of the world of Ideas, we have to ask ourselves, in the first place, why there should be more than one all-embracing Idea and, second, why there should exist a world of *becoming* as well as the world of *being* enshrined in the Ideas. The answer, according to passages in the *Timaeus* that Christian thinkers found relevant to their purposes and interpreted accordingly, is that God (the Christian adaptation of the Platonic "Demiurge") made the world

> because he was good, and in the good no jealousy in any matter can ever arise. So, being without jealousy, he decreed that all things should come as near as possible to being like himself.[15]

In other words, God's purpose is such that it requires, of its very nature, the existence of other beings. Unless he created these beings he would be lacking in a possible attribute, a positive element of perfection. The creation was a natural and spontaneous outpouring of the Divine Being, the result of an innate desire on the part of God to convey upon 'matter,' the primary raw material of creation, all the perfection it was capable of receiving.

The second question follows from the first. How many kinds of temporal and consequently imperfect or incomplete beings must the world contain to answer to this conception of God as creator. The answer, quite simply, is all possible kinds; for, were it to contain less, God's perfection would to that extent fall short:

> What was the living creature in whose likeness he framed the world? We must not suppose that it was any creature that ranks solely as a species: for no copy of that which is incomplete can ever be good. Let us rather say that the world is like, above all things, to that Living Creature of which all other living creatures, severally and in their families, are parts. For that embraces and contains within itself all the intelligible living creatures.[16]

The creation is essentially good, as befits its nature as a reflection of the divine perfection. In its completeness (which is an aspect of its goodness) it contains, not only immortal, supernatural beings—such as the angels of Christian conception—but mortals; for otherwise, "it would not contain all the kinds of living being, as it must if it is to be perfect and complete."[17] From this philosophical position two consequences follow. The first is that the creation is essentially good, insofar as it mirrors the perfection of Being. The second is that its extent and abundance must be as great as the possibility of existence. The world is the better the more beings it contains, and the law of life as it emerges from God's creative intention is a law of fecundity, a law that reflects the expansiveness of the Good.

Bearing this in mind, what is the relationship between "Venus" and "Nature" in Chaucer's poem? Venus, we have seen, lives in a corner of the Garden of Love, and is an ambivalent force within it, combining aspects of life with others that tend to death. "Nature," it would seem, has jurisdiction over the Garden, but the part played in it by "Venus" constitutes a very distinctive problem for the harmony and perfection of the whole. She is, it seems, a force making for death insofar as she stands for the fulfillment of the sensual drive as an end sufficient to itself, unrelated to the creative ends of a providentially directed universe. This is because the sensual drive, so considered, is unable to deal with the realities of time and death, and ends in separation or disappointment.

"Nature," on the other hand, is a force of life in relation to which the same natural impulse is seen in a creative light directed to the engendering of new being and so to completing or maintaining the perfection of a universe that is itself the result of an outpouring of creative love. Love and being are finally words for a single reality, and *love* is the full expression of creative being. This positive, creative aspect of Nature expresses itself in human beings through the institution of marriage, which men and women enter upon to create new being and to achieve such measure of "immortality" as is available to temporal creatures. The ends of "Nature," accordingly, are one with the creative ends of life; those of "Venus," except insofar as she is subject to "Nature," tend on the contrary to its opposite, to death.

Chaucer was not, and did not claim to be, a philosopher, theologian, or metaphysician. He shows, on occasion, a considerable measure of skepticism in relation to these matters. In spite of this they are to no small degree the conditions of his own thinking, and they serve as a foundation at this point for his poem. The ideas came to him, he says (316), showing a proper respect for "authority," through the writings of Alanus de Insulis;[18] but the main influence is no doubt that mediated through the *Roman de la Rose*, the vastly influential allegorical treatment of "love" under all its aspects, first by Guillaume de Lorris and then by Jean de Meun. Chaucer in all probability translated at least a segment of the first part of the poem, that attributed to Guillaume de Lorris, which contains the story of the approach of *L'Amant*, the Lover, to the Garden of Love in search of the object of desire, the Rose, and which tells of the obstacles that he met in this search and of how these were finally overcome by the intervention of Venus, a real, if ambivalent power, whose action in the long second part of the allegory (that written by Jean de Meun) is explored from every point of view.

More precisely, the poem (begun, approximately, in 1237), has two parts. The first is a relatively short section by Guillaume de Lorris, based in its essence on the conceptions of so-called Courtly Love. The lover approaches the Rose at the heart of the Garden. He is wounded by Cupid's arrows and burns with desire to possess the Rose. His suit is opposed by the traditional enemies of Love—by Chastity, by Danger (which we might translate as Disdain, or Stand-offishness), by Shame, and by Wicked Tongue. He is supported by Franchise (Sincerity), by Pity, and by *Belaceuil,* or Fair Welcome. It is clear that, under these forms of allegorical personification an essentially interior drama is being explored. The issue is uncertain, and the conflict for a long period inconclusive. Once, with the help of *Belaceuil* and the favoring intervention of Venus, the Lover succeeds in kissing the Rose; but then *Belaceuil* is imprisoned and the Lover finds himself banished from the Garden.

At this point, the part of the poem attributed to Guillaume de Lorris ends, after constituting in all some 5,000 lines. It is possible that he died when he was nearing the end of the poem as he conceived it. Some forty years later—about 1275—the unfinished work was taken up by Jean de Meun in a spirit that, though not discontinuous with what he found, was in many ways very different. Jean, unlike the court poet Guillaume, was a scholar, philosopher, and a moralist, and he added some 18,000 lines to cover a much vaster plan of his own, in which scientific, philosophical, and satirical elements were combined. The subject of Jean's part of the poem is still "love," but no longer conceived in a courtly or aristocratic spirit; rather "love" as analyzed, satirized, and seen as a natural human impulse directed above all at ensuring the continuity of the species. In this spirit, Chastity is repudiated and women, together with priests, lawyers, and doctors, are ferociously satirized. The satire, however, in a way that answers to a very fundamental dichotomy in medieval thought, also turns upon the repudiation of Chastity. What is seen from one point of view as natural, even as socially necessary if the human species is to maintain itself, is also, and at the same time, a pretext for the satisfaction of selfish and finally destructive appetites. The idea, which seems oddly contradictory to us, is perhaps best considered as a product of the strains, the tensions, that any consistently end-directed, transcendental view of reality is apt to impose upon those who push it to its ultimate consequences.

The *Roman de la Rose,* more particularly as expanded by Jean de Meun, is, or appears to be, a notably digressive poem, though it may be that the unity of underlying purpose is greater than has often been supposed. The main contentions can be simply summarized. It would seem that in the sphere of "Nature," inasmuch as she is left to her own devices, all created beings cooperate, each in its appropriate way in God's creative purposes. The end of these purposes is "generation," the maintenance of the various species into which the creation is divided and the bringing into being of new life as a means of obtaining, within the temporal process, a kind of immortality. It is only when man enters the picture that matters present themselves as more complicated. Man, because he possesses the unique privilege of choice and because, at the same time, he is frequently led astray by passionate forces in himself that are a corruption of the spontaneous life-instinct, separates his desires from "engendrure," the natural expression of creative procreation. The result is a conflict in his nature, which is a main theme of Jean's part of the poem. At the end of it the lover, having overcome with the aid of Venus what his instincts prompt him to see as perverse, anti-life forces of repression, finally achieves the Rose to which he aspires. In so doing, he answers—at least in his own view—to the end of his creation and "Venus" is redeemed by being set in a proper relationship to "Nature".[19]

Chaucer in all probability only translated a part of Guillaume de Lorris's *Roman* (the part called Section A in editions of his work), but he certainly knew the rest of the poem, which remained immensely popular up to the sixteenth century. Though he does not, in the *Parliament*, develop these themes or bring them to anything approaching a conclusion, but rather seems to adopt a notably evasive attitude toward them, they are nevertheless present in the poem. What we are given is a kind of social satire, following a convention in which human pretensions and desires are distanced and divested of undue seriousness by being placed in the mouths of speaking birds.[20] Nature, the "noble emperesse, ful of grace" (319), presides over the rites of St. Valentine's Day, when every natural "fowl" claims his partner, or "make." The stress is on the love of "kynde," natural and procreative, leading to the birth of new life; the passionate desire associated with Venus is seen by contrast, when taken out of its context in the larger design, as sterile and tending to death.

The birds are assembled in a "Parliament," and divided into groups in accordance with their social status. At this point an element of social, even "political" satire makes its entry to modify or extend the preceding matter.[21] What has been authoritatively, theoretically, stated in "earnest" is now subjected to the liberating counterpoise of "game."[22] The poem distinguishes between four principal classes, or—as we might say—"estates," each presented in such a way as gently to undercut their respective pretensions and to underline the element of absurdity that these imply. The "foules of ravyne," natural predators, represent the nobility, and are "hyest set," occupying the highest place in the social order. Next to be mentioned are the "foules smale,"

> That eten, as hem Nature wolde enclyne,
> As worm or thyng of which I telle no tale.
>
> (325–26)

These may be equated, roughly, with what we would call the "bourgeoisie." Next again are the "waterfowl," who may perhaps be taken to represent the greater merchants. Finally, there are the "foul that lyveth by sed" (328), in whom it is possible to see the agricultural class, or—as some have thought—the clergy. The tendency to social satire is evident, though the exact parallels often remain unclear. It is possible, and even likely, that references are intended to actual public issues and events in the poet's own time. After this brief introduction, the members of the various "estates" are more carefully distinguished from one another, as they will be in their interventions later in the story. It should be noted that by no means all the birds are shown as kind or beneficent. As in any human society, elements of good and bad, the kind and the cruel, are intermingled throughout the presentation.

All, however, have come together in response to the "benign" and positive command of Nature, which calls them to fulfill the universal instinct of living things for "marriage" and procreation:

> Of foules every kynde
> That in this world han fetheres and stature
> Men myghten in that place assembled fynde
> Byfor the noble goddesse of Nature,
> And everich of hem dide his besy cure
> Benygnly to chese or for to take,
> By hire acord, his formel or his make.
>
> (365–71)

With the setting thus established, the "debate" begins in the assembled "Parliament." Nature, called now "the vicaire of the almyghty Lord,"

> That hot, cold, hevy, lyght, moyst, and dreye
> Hath knyt by evene noumbres of accord,
>
> (380–1)

opens the discussion. It is she who has disposed the creation, under God's will and in accordance with his design, in a harmonious order or "accord" of parts. She is stated to be, above all, the source of the natural, springtime impulse to mate. As she says to the assembled birds:

> Ye come for to chese—and fle youre wey—
> Youre makes, as I prike yow with plesaunce;
>
> (388–89)

we are reminded in anticipation of the similar impulse celebrated in the opening of the General Prologue to the *Canterbury Tales*.[23]

The debate is to proceed—as befits the auspices under which it is conducted—in due order, an order, however, that, follows a tendency observable elsewhere in Chaucer's work[24] to incline persistently to its opposite. Nature bears on her wrist the "fairest" of creatures, the "formel" eagle, the sum of all possible perfections:

> of shap the gentilleste
> That evere she among hire werkes fond,
> The moste benygne and the goodlieste.
> In hire was everi vertu at his reste,
> So ferforth that Nature hirself hadde blysse
> To loke on hire, and ofte hire bek to kysse.
>
> (373–78)

The assembled company are called upon to witness the choice of a fitting mate for this paragon of aristocratic perfection; and the most noble of birds, the "tercel" eagle, is required, as her natural counterpart, to speak first. Once he has declared his choice and been accepted, each of the other birds is to proceed—still in observance of true "degree"—to choose the "make" that answers to its status and aspirations. This is the *theory* of order that should govern the discussion and reflect the functioning of an ordered society; but what actually happens is, as we shall shortly see, rather different. In the discrepancy between theory and practice, indeed, gently and in no way catastrophically insinuated, lies a principal point of the poem. Finally, it should be noted that free choice *on either side* is to be the essence of the contract. The "formel" who is the object of this competition must be free to agree to the "election" of the suitor who singles her out for his own. Her "freedom" will express itself in an act of generosity (an essential part of the medieval sense of "free") which must itself proceed, on a proper understanding of human possibilities, from an exercise of unconstrained choice.

The "process" begins, then, with the declaration of the "tercel" eagle. He makes his plea in terms of the most exalted values of aristocratic love, as generations of poets have declared them. Speaking "With hed enclyned and with ful humble cheere" (414), he addresses the "formel" as "soverayn lady" and expressly refuses to think of her, in rude, uncourtly terms, as his "fere," or "mate." His offer is made in the language of courtly "service," and he declares that he is ready to die if she rejects him:

> Besekynge hire of merci and of grace,
> As she that is my lady sovereyne;
> Or let me deye present in this place.
>
> (421–23)

In other words, and when due value has been given to the courtliness of the expression, the eagle can be seen to deviate from what the poem assumes to be the true sense of any realistic conception of marriage: a conception that forbids the male to abase himself in pursuit of the love-service and that in no sense requires him to contemplate death as the inevitable end of unrequited love. It is indicative of the contradiction implied in the eagle's plea that, having declared himself in the name of an impossible, indeed an absurd ideal, he nonetheless declares that he alone, among all those present, can be considered worthy to receive the "mercy" he seeks:

> And syn that non loveth hire so wel as I,
> Al be she nevere of love me behette,
> Thanne oughte she be myn thourgh hire mercy,
> For other bond can I non on hire knette.
>
> (435–38)

Chaucer's unobtrusive humor is working here to maintain essential distinctions, to give his bird speaker his due in terms of sentiment and "gentility" while stressing at the same time the unreality that his attitude implies.

The "formel" is abashed by this "idolatrous" approach:

> for shame al wexen gan the hewe
> Of this formel, whan she herde al this.
>
> (444–45)

She is reassured in her embarrassment by her protector Nature before a second eagle intervenes in rivalry with the first. This bird is said to be of "lower kynde" (450), though still within the aristocratic order; and indeed the tone of his argument—the blunt assertion of his greater love—"I love hire bet than ye don, by seint John" (451), the statement that should he be found jealous he is ready to "hangen by the hals" (the neck) (458)—indicates a rougher, less-polished version of the traditional declarations of "service." A third eagle, departing still farther from the courtly norm, brushes aside the entire notion of "service" to affirm his rights of love against all rivals. He points to the real urgency with which

> every foul cryeth out to ben ago
> Forth with his make,
>
> (465–66)

and asserts that even Nature cannot "tarry" to hear half of his declarations in the usual terms. He then disclaims any intention of arguing from the length of his devotion: "Of long servyse avaunte I me nothing" (470), denies that this consideration can be any true measure of the reality of his love, and concludes "at shorte wordes,"

> I wol ben heres, whether I wake or wynke,
> And trewe in al that herte may bethynke.
>
> (482–83)

The effect is that of a return from excessive refinement of sentiment to a more bluntly stated reality that it seeks to conceal under the forms of elaborate and self-conscious make-believe.

The "lesser" birds, indeed, rather like the less "gentle" pilgrims in *The Canterbury Tales*, tend to listen to their "betters" with growing impatience. This expresses itself in a fresh immediacy of speech that stands in significant contrast to the "courtly" terms with which the meeting began. As the third eagle ends his speech, the less genteel fowls protest vividly against what they see as so much pretentious waste of time. "Have don, and lat us wende!", and again, even more emphatically,

> "Come of!" they criede, "allas, ye wol us shende!
> Whan shal youre cursede pleytynge have an ende?"
>
> (494–95)

The discussion collapses, in an unseemly uproar that reflects, not indeed any catastrophic calamity, which would be far removed from the poet's comic intention, but simply the unwillingness of real life to submit to the theoretical ordering within which the most respectable authorities so generously seek to confine it. The final effect amounts to a subversion of the order and decorum originally promoted by Nature herself. In the general confusion the most "plebeian" birds play a vociferous part:

> The goos, the cokkow, and the doke also
> So cryede, "Kek kek! Kokkow! quek quek!" hye,
>
> (498–99)

so much so that the noise went through the dreamer's ears with the effect, we must suppose, of intruding upon his reverie. To this discord is added the sharp comment, at once self-esteeming and compounded with outright common sense, of the goose: "Al this nys not worth a flye!" (501). The "fol kokkow," speaking on behalf of the "worm-fowl," adds his "owene auctorite" in the act of rejecting "authority" itself. Only the turtle-dove, humbly recognizing her own unworthiness—

> I am a sed-foul, oon the unworthieste,
> That wot I wel, and litel of connynge—
>
> (512-13)

puts in a plea for patience against the rising uproar.

Dame Nature, indeed, has a quick ear for the "lewdness" developing around her. She now moves in no uncertain fashion, with "facound," eloquent, and powerful voice, to restore a proper order to the proceedings. She expresses herself with something less than the dignity we might expect from her traditional role. "Hold youre tonges there!", she cries, raising her voice against the surrounding uproar, and moves to restore the limits within which the debate may properly be channeled:

> And I shal sone, I hope, a conseyl fynde
> Yow to delyvere, and fro this noyse unbynde.
> (522–23)

The birds, following due forms of justice, are to appoint representatives to argue their respective points of view and to arrive at a just resolution.

The "legal" phase, so to call it, of the dispute opens under the presidency of Nature. Proper social distinctions are to be observed, so that the "tercelet of the faucoun" (529) is the first to speak in the name of the aristocratic birds. He argues that judgment on the point at issue—"Who loveth best this gentil formel heere"—is hard to give, and that the claims of each suitor are such that it would be difficult to invalidate them. The dispute, he therefore argues, following the assumptions of his kind, may best be resolved on the feudal basis of trial by combat:

> I can not se that argumentes avayle:
> Thanne semeth it there moste be batayle.
> (538–39)

The idea appeals to his social equals, who respond to the prospect of "battle" with enthusiasm. " 'Alredy!' quod these egles tercels tho" (540), but their spokesman does not rest his contention there, pointing out that he has not finished stating his position, which turns out to be the argument already put forward by the first suitor, the "royal tercel" of lines 393 and 415: that his length of "service" gives him a prior right in the case. In his "aristocratic" way he regards the superior merit of his "client" as obvious and expects it to be recognized as such. "And therefore pes," he concludes,

> Me wolde thynke how that the worthieste
> Of knyghthod, and lengest had used it,
> Most of estat, of blod the gentilleste,
> Were sittyngest for hire, if that hir leste:
> And of these thre she wot hireself, I trowe,
> Which that he be, for it is light to knowe."
> (548–53)

The assumption of superiority, and the dismissal of other arguments as irrelevant, answer admirably to the urbane comic intention.

As the other birds add their voices to the debate, the "dramatic" quality of the exchange—always a sign of Chaucer's deepening involvement in his conceptions—very notably quickens. The goose, designated to speak for the waterfowl on account of her ready tongue, begins with a self-important "kakelynge" and produces a common-sense solution of which she is evidently proud:

> She seyde, "Pes! now tak kep every man,
> And herkeneth which a resoun I shal forth brynge!
> My wit is sharp, I love no taryinge;
> I seye I rede hym, though he were my brother,
> But she wol love hym, lat hym love another!"
>
> (563–67)

To her mind this solution is obvious and satisfying; but the sparrowhawk, as a lesser aristocratic bird, expresses disdain both for the reasoning and for the kind of speaker who has produced it. "Lo, here a parfit resoun of a goos!"

> It lyth nat in his wit, ne in his wille,
> But soth is seyd, "a fol can not be stille."
>
> (573–74)

The remark rouses the "gentil" fowls to approving laughter; but it remains unsupported by argument, and the "seed-fowl" call on the turtle-dove to advance their point of view.

The dove puts in a bashful, and quite unaristocratic plea for the "romantic" virtue of constancy in love. Blushing "for shame al red," she says "Nay, God forbede a lovere shulde chaunge!" and goes on to plead

> Though that his lady everemore be straunge,
> Yit lat hym serve hire ever, til he be ded."
>
> (584–85)

She also stresses the need for constancy in love: "I wol ben hires, til that the deth me take" (588). This, we might say, is an assertion of the aristocratic virtues through a sentimental "bourgeois" voice; and it invites the impatience of the duck, which quacks its disapproval of so much romanticism:

> "Wel bourded," quod the doke, "by myn hat!
> That men shulde loven alwey causeles,
> Who can a resoun fynde or wit in that?

> Daunseth he murye that is myrtheles?
> Who shulde recche of that is recheles?
> Ye quek!" yit seyde the doke, ful wel and fayre,
> "There been mo sterres, God wot, than a payre!"
>
> (589–95)

The aristocratic party, however, have no use for this kind of realism. "Now fy, cherl!" says the "gentil" tercelet, "Out of the donghil cam that word ful right!" (597). The duck is dismissed as too gross to have any proper understanding of the matters under discussion:

> Thy kynde is of so low a wrechednesse
> That what love is, thow canst nat seen ne gesse.
>
> (601–2)

The last word, however, does not rest with this dismissal. The cuckoo, representing the "worm-eaters," declares itself indifferent concerning the entire dispute as long as it gets what it wants:

> "So I," quod he, "may have my make in pes,
> I reche nat how longe that ye stryve.
> Lat ech of hem be soleyn al here lyve,"
>
> (605–7)

a comment that once more moves the more refined birds—among them the "merlin," another of the lesser birds of "rapine"—to turn on its proponent as "mortherere of the heysoge on the braunche" (612), as "rewthlesse glotoun," and as an essentially "soleyn"—solitary, anti-social—"wormes corrupcioun."

The episode amounts to a delicate and balanced exercise in social satire, one from which no position is excepted and which ends, as Chaucerian attempts to assert the necessity of social order are apt to do, in the subversion of order and its substitution by something that resembles chaos. To Nature it seems that the threat of anarchy has not been removed and she intervenes to set matters right by an assertion of authority. "Now pes," quod Nature, "I comaunde heer!" (617). She proposes that the "formel," as object of contention, should be allowed to make her choice in freedom. "Thus juge I, Nature, for I may not lye" (629). Her judgment is delivered in accordance with the true reality of things. She goes on to say, however, that *reason*, if reason were relevant in matters of love, would lead the "formel" to choose the "tercel" as a fitting mate, for as such nature herself created him:

> Which I have wrought so wel to my plesaunce,
> That to yow hit oughte to been a suffisaunce.
>
> (636–37)

The "formel," in reply, accepts this judgment—

> My rightful lady, goddesse of Nature!
> Soth is that I am evere under youre yerde,
> As is everich other creature—
>
> (639–41)

but asks further for "respit for to avise me" (648).[25] She rejects the insecure service of Venus and Cupid, but declines for the moment to enter into a formal commitment. Nature accepts her decision, which leaves the other birds free to choose their mates and to fly away without delay. Turning to the eagle suitors, she advises them to exercise the patience that her judgment and a sense of reality both impose. "A yer is nat so longe to endure" (661) and, in the meantime, she suggests that the "formel" is well quit of their inopportune attentions.

Each bird, then, chooses his or her "make" in accordance with the promptings of its nature, and all are left content in their submission to the universal "law of kynde":

> And whan this werk al brought was to an ende,
> To every foul Nature yaf his make
> By evene acord, and on here way they wende,
> And, Lord, the blisse and joye that they make!
> For ech of hem gan other in wynges take,
> And with here nekkes ech gan other wynde,
> Thankynge alwey the noble goddesse of kynde.
>
> (666–72)

The poem ends with a celebration of Nature as source of life. The birds confirm this by singing a "roundel" (680–92) that affirms the victory of spring over the death of winter. The "longe nyghtes blake" of winter deprivation are over for all living things and the sun of summer has returned in affirmation of the triumph of life. The poet, awakening from his dream, is left to return to his reading of yet "othere bokes" and to look forward hopefully—though, perhaps, without excessive conviction—to further and more adequate understanding:

> I wok, and othere bokes tok me to,
> To reede upon, and yit I rede alwey.
> I hope, ywis, to rede so som day
> That I shal mete som thyng for to fare
> The bet, and thus to rede I nyl nat spare.
>
> (695–99)

The conclusion is inconclusive in a very Chaucerian way. We have been left, perhaps, with the sense of a poem divided into two parts that do not hang together with complete consistency. The first half, making use of the dream convention to advance a traditional "philosophy" of Nature, seems to coexist uneasily with the vividly human tones and stressed particularity of the bird-debate to which it leads. If this is so, and if Chaucer at the end of his poem felt less than satisfied with what he had achieved, this did not lead him to leave it, like *The House of Fame*, open-ended or finally incomplete. He announces rather his intention to return to the reading that represents for him the "authority" that, once allied to "experience," may lead him to "fare the better," to conceive poems that may reflect more adequately his effort to marry the two terms of his concern—those represented by authority and experience—in a more living way, so as to answer more convincingly to his developing sense of what a poem might be.

5
Troilus and Criseyde

1

All the Chaucerian poems we have so far considered are, each in its own way, tentative performances. The reasons for this can be reduced to two. There is a sense that the language at the poet's disposal is an imperfect instrument, that it still has to reach a state in which the "great" themes of classical literature could be expressed with adequate force and dignity, and there is a related feeling that the conventions that his age offered to the poet have proved less than sufficient to express the purposes developing in his mind in the process of writing. More particularly, the "dream" device, which Chaucer had used to explore his sense of the relationship between "authority" and "experience," tradition and novelty, has failed to answer to his growing sense of the rich and various unpredictability of real human living.

Nothing of this kind can be said of *Troilus and Criseyde,* a poem that in its scale and carefully planned structure seems to dispel all doubts of this nature. Chaucer, we feel, is at last confident of his ability to write a poem answering to his own sense of "classical" completeness and universality. The subject is a derivation from one of the most familiar medieval tales, a tale, moreover, that has the added attraction of bringing the imagination back to the great issues of life and death as worked out in the story of Troy. Based on a passing reference in the *Iliad,* taken up into the wider Trojan theme as developed by a series of lesser authors writing in the so-called Dark Ages, celebrated and transformed by French court poets and Italian translators from the end of the twelfth century onward, it had been, by Chaucer's own time, incorporated by Boccaccio into his *Filostrato* to become the principal source of the poem.

Chaucer's treatment of the story, which has been described as a "medievalizing" of Boccaccio's material,[1] is marked by the fusion of two main elements. The first is a development of the courtly convention of love as aristocratic service, and of the lover as one who is bound by the force of his passion to pursue an end that, because it is by its nature incapable of inserting itself into the societal context of marriage, becomes finally hopeless. The second adapts the ever-present reality of the war of Troy to the medieval idea of tragedy as dependent on the turn of Fortune's wheel, so that the successive stages of Troilus's story take him in the carefully marked stages of an ascending and descending narrative curve that covers the development of the poem's five books "Fro wo to wele, and after out of joie" (1.4), following the stages of a process seen to be implicit in the very nature of sublunary reality.

Both these elements are related, in the proem to the first book, to the poet's attitude to his material. He presents himself as one dedicated by the very nature of his undertaking to the God of Love: "I, that God of Loves servantz serve" (15). As such he is committed to inviting sympathy for a hero whose fortunes will be determined throughout by the compelling nature of this service. He is careful to add, however, in a gesture that comes effectively from an author, or translator, who is to be thought of as reading his poem and who deprecates any claim to excessive importance, that he has no personal experience in these matters and that he does not for his "unliklynesse" (16) even pray to the "god" he serves for success in his unfamiliar enterprise.

Even in his inexperience, however, he will be obliged in the course of his narration to come to terms with the unhappy nature of the story as his "source" presents it. This prompts him to seek support in a double prayer to the effect that those who, like his hero, have not been favored by fortune in their loves should be brought "*in hevene* to solas" (31) and that he himself should receive from "God so dere" the power to tell the "peyne and wo" of Troilus's luckless or "unsely aventure" (34–35). Already, in this use of language that carries specifically religious implications, there is the suggestion of a double vision, which the language of the poem, answering to the retelling of a pagan story by a Christian poet for a Christian audience, will persistently reflect. The heaven that the narrator desires for unhappy lovers, and that is the gift of "love" to those whom it deigns to favor, shadows that of the "God so dere" from whom the poet, who shares with his audience in a truth not available to his pagan source, begs for support in the telling of his story.

The two orders—those of pagan love and Christian Charity—are interwoven in this opening. The service of the God of Love is conceived in terms that echo Christian concepts:

> And biddeth ek for hem that ben at ese,
> That God hem graunte ay good perseveraunce,
> And sende hem myght hire ladies so to plese
> That it to Love be worship and plesaunce.
>
> (43–46)

By praying for those "that Loves servauntz be," the poet narrator says that he is in hope to "advance" the saving of his soul and to "lyve in charite" (47–49). By adopting this tone Chaucer allows himself to combine the appearance of almost naive sympathy with a certain ironic detachment. He will encourage us, by his use of the convention, at once involving and distancing, of the narrator[2] to share, or at least sympathetically to understand the situation of one who declares himself to be the servant of the servants of the God of Love, even to the degree of sharing the assumptions of the code that governs the behavior of lovers according to the accepted poetic models; but he will also maintain his freedom to recognize the point at which the service will turn, in the necessary nature of things, from "wo to wele," indeed, but "after out of joye." Love, as the poem will declare it, is conceived as valuable and ennobling, as constituting a genuine civilizing force upon human lives; but, accepting this, we are also required to see that it passes; that exclusive dedication to it can be personally degrading; and that its end—thus unilaterally pursued—can only lie in disappointment and tragedy.

The claims of reasonable reality are asserted as soon as we pass from the proem to the first lines of the poem. The story to be told is given its setting in the siege of Troy, the course of which will condition the fortunes of the lovers and eventually determine their fate. It is important, more especially, that the background to this tale of love is one in which betrayal plays a part—important, because the love will itself end in a betrayal. Calkas, Criseyde's father and "a great divine" in Troy, has learned from the god Apollo that his city is inexorably doomed, "wolde whoso nolde" (77). From the first we are made aware of the existence of forces that, operating through the "stars," limit personal freedom of choice. To escape from this doom Calkas has fled from his native city, leaving his daughter behind him in Troy under the shadow of his betrayal.[3]

With the ground prepared in this way we are introduced to the hero at the moment of his "conversion" to the love "service." The setting is the Trojan feast of "Palladion," which coincides with April,

> whan clothed is the mede
> With newe grene, of lusty Veer the pryme,
> And swote smellen floures white and rede:
>
> (156–58)

a time when, as all readers of poetry know, "many a lusty knyght" and "many a lady fressh and mayden bright" are arrayed "bothe for the seson and the feste" (165–68). Against this setting, at once attractively alive and steeped in literary convention, we are shown Troilus leading his band of young men—"his yonge knyghtes"—idly "up and doun" in "thilke large temple,"

> Byholding ay the ladies of the town,
> Now here, now there; for no devocioun
> Hadde he to non:
>
> (186–88)

arrogantly and superciliously observing the young women and their foolish admirers. The scene is familiar, both in terms of poetic convention and of real life. The "temple" could be any large collegiate church crowded at the late morning hour for the fashionable sunday Mass, and Troilus is both a figure of youthful chivalry grafted onto the Trojan tale and a young man riding for a fall. In the very moment of congratulating himself on his superiority to the normal human condition—"Loo! is this naught wisely spoken?" (205)—his eye falls on Criseyde and he is reduced by the power emanating from her eyes to helpless servitude.

Once again the situation rests on an established poetic tradition. We know, because generations of poets have told us, that the God of Love has power to deal with this kind of presumption:

> he that now was moost in pride above,
> Wax sodeynly moost subgit unto love.
>
> (230–31)

Experience shows that "may no man fordon the lawe of kynde" (238). Those who assert their superiority to this "law" stand properly condemned for their presumption and Chaucer, commenting with exquisite comedy in the person of his narrator, compares his hero's plight to that of a horse driven by a crack of his master's whip to recognize his equine subjection to the "law of kynde":

> As proude Bayard gynneth for to skippe
> Out of the weye, so pryketh hym his corn,
> Til he a lasshe have of the longe whippe:
> Than thynketh he, "Though I praunce al byforn
> First in the trays, ful fat and newe shorn,
> Yet am I but an hors, and horses lawe
> I moot endure, and with my feres drawe."
>
> (218–24)

In comparing Troilus's unforeseen situation to that of a beast in harness, Chaucer is indicating—gently and humorously, without a trace of moralizing superiority—both the rashness of his neglect of the laws of "nature" and the subjection of the reasonable human self into which it leads those who are unprepared for its devastating onset.

This does not mean that we are to withhold all assent from what the surface of the narrative implies. Having insinuated its comment on the dangers implied in surrender to the power of "love," the poem reaffirms the positive effects of that passion as the poets have traditionally seen them. Love, we are told, "ofte"

> hath the cruel herte apesed,
> And worthi folk maad worthier of name,
> And causeth moost to dreden vice and shame.
>
> (250–52)

It is no part of the poem's intention to deny their proper value to the civilizing powers implied in the love convention. The final comment, true to its deepest sense, is a blend of understanding and irony that avoids the extremes both of cynicism and of sentimentality. Since the force of love may not "goodly"—that is, in right and natural behavior—"be withstode," men and women do well to accept it in realistic recognition of the natural facts. As experience shows,

> The yerde is bet that bowen wole and wynde
> Than that that brest.
>
> (257–58)

To ask whether we are to accept this idea as it stands (for it is after all the narrator's and we have reason to suspect that some of his judgments are conditioned by his desire to see things as he would have them be), or to see in it an ironic insinuation of connivance with moral weakness, is to be very close to the intention that gives final depth and validity to Chaucer's poem.

All this prepares for the *coup de foudre* that both the convention and the poet's purpose require. Seized by this "sudden" vision, Troilus looks at Criseyde more closely—"in thrifty wise" (275)—and, as he does so, his heart is stirred and he sighs in the soft dissimulation that this kind of love requires:

> "O mercy, God," thoughte he, "wher hastow woned,
> That art so feyr and goodly to devise?"
> Therwith his herte gan to sprede and rise,
> And softe sighed, lest men myghte hym here,
> And caught ayeyn his firste pleyinge chere.
>
> (276–80)

Criseyde's reaction to this unexpected and carefully camouflaged approach stresses her beauty and femininity—"creature / Was nevere lasse mannysshe in semynge" (283–84)—as well as the mixture of diffidence and defiance in her response:

> To Troilus right wonder wel with alle
> Gan for to like hire mevynge and hire chere,
> Which somdel deignous was, for she let falle
> Hire look a lite aside in swich manere,
> Ascaunces. "What! may I nat stonden here?"
>
> (288–92)

The situation is beautifully caught in terms of that grasp of character in action which is the extreme, even in a contemporary context, the revolutionary achievement of Chaucer's poem. Aware of her uneasy situation as an unprotected widow and daughter of a traitor, the young woman stands her ground with a touch of defiance and in full awareness of her assets. By the end of this wordless encounter confusion has entered the young man's mind. He feels the need to renounce his former arrogance. Like a snail aware of danger "He was tho glad his hornes in to shrinke" (300) as, in more explicitly romantic terms, he sensed "dyen . . . the spirit in his herte" (306–7). The narrator, true to his position as the servant of Love's devotees, is left to celebrate the downfall of youthful presumption as the just revenge of life itself. "Blissed be Love, that kan thus folk converte" (308). Once again the recourse to a religious analogy answers to the essentially double vision that so effectively prevails in the tale. As Troilus leaves the temple his attitude has become that of a convert who contemplates the object of his new-found devotion with a sense of his own unworthiness, whose life, far from being infused with the sense of happiness that this change might have been expected to produce in him, has been invaded by a "woe" that his social standing requires him to "dissimulen and hide" (322).

Woe, indeed, largely prevails in Troilus as the first result of his sentimental conversion and of the concealment to which it leads. Left to his own devices he sighs and groans on his bed—throughout his unhappy story he will show a readiness to seek refuge there—as he tries to recall Criseyde in his daydreams. Love brings him to a condition of "sickness" (489), which is very unlike the state of "grace" ambiguously proposed to love's devotees in their romantic self-absorption. His heart bleeds in uncertainty and "dread" (499–502) and he can even think of death as "a gret comfort" (528), a relief from the fear of being "byjaped" (531), betrayed and turned into an object of ridicule by the very force of his passion.

The convention that provides the poem with its point of departure stipulates that societal restraints prevent the lover from declaring himself openly. He needs a go-between, and this gives Chaucer the opportunity to develop, in the person of Criseyde's uncle Pandarus, the most original character in the poem. Vastly developed from Boccaccio's straightforwardly cynical companion, Pandarus becomes an older man who incorporates into his person many of the features of *L'Ami*, the worldly wise counselor of the Lover in the *Romaunt of the Rose*. Like the Friend, Pandarus believes that love is a positive good, inherent in human nature and well worth the enjoying; but, also like *L'Ami*, he believes that the lover may have to practice deception, or at least to indulge in a measure of subtle maneuvering, to obtain the end he sincerely desires for his protégé. The part he plays in what ends as a story of betrayal should not persuade us to see him entirely in a negative light. There are moments—especially in the earlier part of the poem—when we seem to hear in his comments something not altogether unlike his creator's own voice, alternately tolerant and gently skeptical. He emerges from Chaucer's portrayal as at once experienced and sentimental, genuinely open to the human compulsion of love and personally unsuccessful in its pursuit, apt—this more dubiously—to seek satisfaction by promoting the achievement of others and to find in his anticipation of the pleasures of the moment as experienced by them the end to which all life—"nature," in his reading of it—tends.

This ambivalence emerges only gradually in Pandarus's early exchanges with Troilus. As his efforts on behalf of his friend begin to take shape, he is seen to be both the mouthpiece for a conception of love celebrated as natural and life-giving (this is the way the narrator, as servant of the God of Love, tends to see him) and a voice of temptation wooing Troilus from his responsible manhood; both the kindly and mature uncle, solicitous for the happiness of his niece and his friend, and—at the same time—the artful and engrossed manipulator of feeling who derives a certain vicarious enjoyment from the relationship he is so busily promoting and from the exercise of his own role in advancing it. Moved in this way, and reflecting some of the attributes of the serpent-tempter in the Garden of Innocence—for a sense of the Fall as a central reality in all human life is never far from the medieval imagination—Pandarus, promoting what he sees as the natural pursuit of love's happiness, will end by calling the hero away from the obligations of his reasonable moral self and lead him into subjection to the promptings of his lower nature.

The spectacle of his friend's unhappiness moves Pandarus initially to a typical gush of sentiment—he "neigh malt for wo and routhe" (582)—and, beyond it, to a common-sense reproof of such perversity. To counter it he makes a repeated appeal to friendship—"Now frend" "To hiden from thi frend" (584, 587)—and to the confidence that it should inspire.

He also draws, again like *L'Ami*, on the fund of proverbial wisdom that is always at his disposal. The proverbs to which he appeals tend to be double-edged beyond his immediate intention. When he tries to encourage Troilus by asserting that the blind can walk safely where those who see fall (628), or when he suggests that "often wise men ben war by foolys" (635), we are bound to question the advantages of "blindness" and "folly" as safe guides in the conduct of life. Pandarus stresses, reasonably enough, that "trust," confidence in one's fellows, is an attribute of human "truth"—the two words *trust* and *truth* are indeed inseparable from one another in their final meaning—and a necessary aspect of any valid life:

> to trusten som wight is a preve
> Of trouth;
>
> (690–91)

but the possibility that trust may be misplaced remains and events will show that reliance on Pandarus's superior "experience" will bring his friend to an end very different from that which the claim to "realism" so plausibly advanced proposes as attainable.

Not surprisingly, Troilus rejects these counsels as irrelevant to his condition. "Lat be thyne olde ensaumples" (760), he rejoins, clinging to his determination to see himself, somewhat sententiously, as "refus of every creature" (570). Pandarus replies, once more reasonably enough, by pouring scorn on this emotional excess and by appealing to his young friend to be "fressh and grene" (816) in the life-giving service of love. The recurrence at this point of Chaucer's favorite epithets expressing the reaction of men to the vernal impulses of reborn life alerts us to the presence of powerful and, up to a point, positive feeling behind Pandarus's devices. They are sufficient to move Troilus—not least because he is being led where he wants to go—to cast himself upon his friend's counsel. "Allas!" he says, resting his reliance upon the older man's resources, "what is me best to do?" (828). Finally, urged to follow nature by bringing his love into the open, he confesses on the point of swooning away that the "swete fo" (874) who so exclusively dominates his being is Criseyde.

At this crucial point, as Troilus dedicates himself to the pursuit of love, the poem introduces for the first time the larger philosophical themes that govern its course. He responds to Pandarus's offer of help by declaring himself convinced that Fortune is his "foe" (837). Pandarus argues that the influence of the "goddess" is common to all men. He further asserts that as it is her nature to bring joy to sorrow, so she will in due course, and by an equally inevitable turn of the wheel, convert sorrow into joy. His expression of this argument rests on commonplaces of medieval thinking that derive ultimately, like most of Chaucer's "philosophical" statements, from Boethius:[4]

> Quod Pandarus. "Than blamestow Fortune
> For thow art wroth; ye, now at erst I see.
> Woost thow nat wel that Fortune is comune
> To everi manere wight in som degree?
> And yet thow hast this comfort, lo, parde,
> That, as hire joies moten overgon,
> So mote hire sorwes passen everechon."
>
> (841–47)

"Lo, parde": the sense of the worldly-wise mentor pulling this speculative rabbit out of his conjuror's hat should not obscure from us the presence of a finally specious element in the encouragement offered. In what follows Pandarus develops his theme to his own ends:

> For if hire whiel stynte any thyng to torne,
> Than cessed she Fortune anon to be.
> Now, sith hire whiel by no way may sojourne,
> What woostow if hire mutabilite
> Right as thyselven list, wol don by the,
> Or that she be naught fer fro thyn helpynge?
> Paraunter thow hast cause for to synge.
>
> (848–54)

The gist of the argument in orthodox terms is clear. The affairs of men in the temporal order are subject to the operations of a power—rationalized and personified as "Fortune"—which presents itself as fickle and changeable to their limited, time-conditioned understanding. Experience shows that what "Fortune" gives at one moment a corresponding turn of the "wheel" will take away at the next. This reality has, in terms of orthodox thinking, a positive purpose, which men may not always be ready to understand. It ensures that the temporal goods that they enjoy, and that they should strive to deserve by the exercise of responsible moral choice, do not become the undeserved and fixed monopoly of any man or social group;[5] and it also teaches them not to place their ultimate desire upon what is of its nature changeable and impermanent. The last truth will prove to have its relevance for Troilus's understanding of love; but Pandarus, in pursuit of his immediate ends, reads it in the light of an easy and illusory optimism. If Troilus, he argues, now finds himself unhappy, he can expect that the very Fortune that has brought him to this condition will, in the course of her further working, raise him from despair to felicity. What he does *not* say, but what will emerge with desolate clarity in the course of the story, is that any happiness conceived on these lines must be subject to impermanence. The wheel will continue to turn and the most men can hope for, on these terms, is an unending succession of pointless alternatives.

These are general "philosophical" speculations, backed by a weight of "authoritative" argument. In a poem they are justified, not as abstractions but through the presentation of human character and motive in action. It seems proper at this point to attempt an assessment of the part played by Pandarus in this story. This will not be simple or onesided. Not by any means *all* of his advice is to be regarded as perverse. When he tells Troilus not to wallow in his sorrow like a pig in clover,[6] his is the voice of common sense and humanity. He is right to tell his friend that it is senseless to talk of dying for love without making his feelings known, and still more right to stress that love is natural, positive, and openly to be declared:

> naught but good it is
> To loven wel, and in a worthy place;
> The oughte nat to clepe it hap, but grace.
>
> (894–6)

All this is true *as far as it goes*. The moral crux of the story, and the key to Pandarus's place in it, lies largely in that necessary qualifying phrase. He believes that a refusal to recognize "the law of kynde"—expressed in terms of natural, human, physical love where this is worthily offered—amounts not only to a failure in common sense, but to a kind of "sin." It is perhaps at this point that we begin to see where he will fail his friend. His attitude leads less to a proper understanding of the place of love in life than to an equivocal confusion concerning its nature, a confusion that is implicit in his recourse to the word *grace* and that induces the "romantic" sentimentalist to see things as they are not and to end by invoking friendship, the supreme expression of human "truth," to advance treachery and self-deception.

Throughout this story two orders of love—the "natural" and the "celestial"—shadow one another in a constantly shifting play of relationships. It is Pandarus's limitation to seek to advance the partial vision to the exclusion of the reality that finally justifies it. This is not a matter of simply opposing "charity" to "love of kynde," or of affirming one truth at the expense of the other. That would have produced a poem more didactically conceived, notably less alive and intelligent than what Chaucer has given us. The finally simple reality, as this story requires us to see it, is that "love of kynde" passes, that only insofar as it can be seen as a proper, a natural and fully human extension of the order of "charity"—an extension at once nurtured and limited by its temporal foundation—can it be said to have meaning or value. Recognition of the existence and validity of the spiritual guarantees, in the world that the poet's "philosophy" postulates as answering to the reality of human experience, the value of its temporal reflection. This is presented in the poem as a reality that it is Pandarus's limitation not to be able to see or understand for what it is. His optimistic conclusion—"so we may ben gladed alle thre"—is arrived at by blurring necessary distinctions in the name of a comfortable, a finally complaisant vision of the complex and interrelated concerns of what the poet—if not, initially, the story as given by his "source"—requires us to see as a central and realistic human truth.

By the end of the first book Troilus has entrusted his entire being to his friend's care: "My lif, my deth, hol in thyn hond I leye" (1053). He has made a choice that will lead him, beyond the immediate achievement of his desire, to his final tragedy. This is not to say, lest we succumb to an overly moralistic reading of his story, that he is not granted in full measure the virtues that belong to his kind of love:

> For he bicom the frendlieste wight,
> The gentilest, and ek the mooste fre,
> The thriftiest and oon the beste knyght,
> That in his tyme was or myghte be.
> Dede were his japes and his cruelte,
> His heighe port and his manere estraunge,
> And eech of tho gan for a vertu chaunge.
>
> (1079–85)

Under the influence of his commitment Troilus, according to the "source," has been subjected to a refining, an essentially "civilizing" process that it is no part of the poet's purpose, as he records it, to belittle. *Friendliness*, celebrated as the central human "truth" it is recognized to be, implies a good deal more than we might initially be inclined to read into the word. To be a worthy *friend* is to fulfill an important part of the social, trusting nature on which a fully human life depends: and *gentilest* and *fre* (or "generous") are words to which a poetic tradition has given the depth and weight that are recognized to belong to them. Nor is there any doubt about the seriousness of the blemishes that the hero, who so recently exhibited them in the "temple," has been led to renounce—the adolescent "japes" and self-satisfied "cruelty," the arrogance and the "manere estraunge" that governed his conduct before Criseyde entered his consciousness. A real "conversion" to the "vertu" of love's devotion has been practiced in Troilus, and we are not to undervalue its validity because the language that expresses it may strike us as remote or unreal. Having recognized this important truth, however, we must also see that Troilus remains at heart "a man that hurt is soore" (1087), one whose state Pandarus has indeed alleviated—"ylissed wel"—but one whom, beyond this, he has "heeled no deel moore" (1089).

The return to Criseyde at the opening of the second book brings with it a very notable quickening of the narrative tempo. The opening book has been largely concerned with the predicament of Troilus as a result of his unexpected surrender to the power of love; and, though he is without doubt the hero of this tragedy, there has been something passive, even at times approaching the absurd, in the presentation of his emotional condition. By moving Criseyde to her central position in the story, and by concentrating on the efforts of Pandarus to bring the pair together, Chaucer introduces into his poem an entirely new range of possibilities, which can properly be called "dramatic." As the pace of the action quickens, mainly in connection with Pandarus's increasingly breathless to-and-fro movement between the lovers, and as Criseyde is shown debating within herself the contrary impulses that her delicate situation in Troy imposes, we become aware—perhaps for the first time in English literature—of characters who are no longer set against one another in solid descriptive blocks, but who are seen as it were in various ranges of perspective, interacting upon one another and achieving the full measure of their human potentiality in relation to the developing narrative.[7]

Criseyde has already been introduced—albeit in passing—in the opening stages of the first book. We have been shown a young woman who possesses the familiar attributes of the courtly mistress—"Honor, estaat, and wommanly noblesse" (1. 287)—and who is both uncertain of herself and almost defiantly conscious of the advantages that her womanly condition can give her. Given the social arrangements that the poem takes for granted, she and her lover are not in a position to declare their feelings openly, so that an outside influence is needed to bring them together.

That influence is provided, at the opening of the second book, by the entrance of Pandarus, which—as we have already had occasion to see[8]—brings with it a notable quickening of leisurely narrative by the cut and thrust of direct, double-edged dialogue. Addressing his niece in the name of "nature" in its springtime manifestation—"May, that moder is of monthes glade" (2. 50)—he calls upon her to throw off her widow's weeds, and by so doing to flaunt the proprieties of respectable society—and to dance:

> But yet, I say, ariseth, lat us daunce,
> And cast youre widewes habit to mischaunce!
> What list yow thus youreself to disfigure,
> Sith yow is tid thus fair an aventure?
>
> (221–24)

It is the poet's intention to bring us to respond to what is natural and spontaneous in the attitudes of Pandarus as well as and at the same time as, to see what is specious in his pleadings. As he bursts in upon Criseyde's seclusion—the benevolent middle-aged uncle with a jolly tune on his lips and a flower in his buttonhole—we can see in him a reflection of one of the most persistent of the minor pagan deities: Priapus,[9] in his double aspect of garden-dweller, promoter of husbandry, and symbol of the animal lust that lurks in the dark corners of the garden, domesticated indeed, even by his own wry admission unsuccessful in his pursuit of love,[10] but ready to satisfy vicariously the needs that his own performance cannot placate.

The whole poem, indeed, balances these opposed realities against one another, achieving in the process comic effects and psychological insights of a rarely satisfying kind. As Pandarus prepares the ground for delivering the message on the tip of his tongue, the situation between uncle and niece is full of unspoken motives on either side. An intricate game of social chess, involving a web of situations tacitly recognized and deliberately withheld, is being played out between contenders who are keenly aware of the implications, declared and undeclared, of each move and countermove on the board. Criseyde is fearful and anxious to hear what is being held back from her:

> Both I am agast what ye wol seye,
> And ek me longeth it to wite, ywys.
>
> (311–12)

As he prepares to deliver his tidings "she gan hire eighen down to caste, / And Pandarus to coghe gan a lite" (253–54). A moment later, as he is asking himself how he can most tactfully bring out what he has to say, we are told that he

> loked on hire in a bysi wyse,
> And she was war that he byheld hire so,
> And seyde, "Lord! so faste ye m'avise!
> Sey ye me nevere er now—What sey ye, no?"
>
> (274–77)

It would be wrong to think that his motives at this point are entirely devious. Throughout the poem he is at pains to deny that he is a "bawd"[11], claims to be acting in accordance with an honorable conception of love, and urges his niece to take pity on her lover and to treat him in accordance with the recognized laws that govern the conduct of "love" in this society. We are not to take his words entirely at their own value, if only because we are aware that the motives of men are not always what they claim to be and because we know how this story will end; but neither shall we deny a proper measure of human sympathy for his defense of what he sees as the "natural" conduct of human life.

The presentation of Criseyde's position is equally penetrating. She is ready to follow her uncle in finding it natural to love and in seeing Troilus as both "gentle" and "the king's son." She is also aware that to refuse the advances of this desirable and powerful suitor may, given her insecure position in Troy, bring her into "worse plight." The presentation of her internal debate is remarkably real in its effect. Immediately after Pandarus has taken his leave, having planted the seed of his intrigue, we see her grasping at the confidence she needs by an argument that the course of her later history will negate:

> For man may love, of possibilite,
> A womman so, his herte may tobreste,
> And she naught love ayein, but if hire leste.
> (607–9)

Scarcely has this been spoken, "as she sat allone, and thoughte thus" (610), Troilus rides past her window, returning from a victorious encounter with the Greek enemy. The sight of him "So lik a man of armes and a knyght . . . fulfilled of heigh prowesse" (631–32) marks the moment in her history that corresponds to Troilus's surrender in the "temple." It is given with the same sense of an irresistible power acting upon human frailty:

> Criseyda gan al his chere aspien,
> And leet it so softe in hire herte synke,
> That to hireself she seyde, "Who yaf me drynke?"
> (649–51)

This is the love potion, which bears within it an element of poison and which represents in poetic tradition the other, the death-directed face of desire. Although Criseyde has just expressed her confidence in her ability to refrain from surrender to the power of this potent draught unless she wills her assent—"but if hire leste"—the course of her story will show that it is the nature of the compulsion to which men and women have given the name of "love" to take them out of themselves, leading them beyond where they may initially have wished to go. For some time to come Criseyde will seek to evade recognition of this uneasy truth, trying to persuade herself that there is nothing binding or dangerous in the new reality that has so unexpectedly and so powerfully forced itself upon her, and clinging to the advantages she perceives in her freedom as one of the "fairest" and "goodliest," "so men seyn, in al the town of Troie" (746–49). The result is to lead her to argue, with a brave show of confidence,

> I am myn owene womman, wel at ese,
> I thank it God, as after myn estat,
> Right yong, and stonde unteyd in lusty leese,
> Withouten jalousie or swich debat:
> Shal noon housbonde seyn to me "chek mat!"
>
> (750–54)

In truth, however she may seek to deny the fact in her uneasy self-communings, the die is cast, and what follows is directed, beyond its wealth of human aspiration and pathos, to a tragic conclusion.

Behind these attempts at buttressing her self-esteem there lies a deep-seated insecurity that one part of Criseyde's mind is realistic enough to recognize. She *fears* that this new power may place "in jeopardy" the "sikernesse" and "libertee" (771–73) she cherishes. Love presents itself to her thought as a compound of "mistrust" and "strife" (780) and it seems to her only too likely that the lot of women is, realistically considered, their "owen wo to drynke" (784). These ominous misgivings lead her to seek relief in "pleye" (812), in the seclusion of the garden where, in a deliberately romantic abstraction from the world of real pressures and difficult choices, her sister "Antigone the shene" (824) (the "bright," the "fair," beautiful beyond the common visions of earth) sings to celebrate the power of Love as a source of beauty and virtue in a voice "that an hevene . . . was to here" (826). Her song of vibrant nostalgia raises the exalted courtly virtues to an almost Platonic vision of perfect beauty, a shadowing, at once moving and ambiguous, of supernatural "charity" and Christian grace:

> O Love, to whom I have and shal
> Ben humble subgit, trewe in myn entente,
> As I best kan, to yow, lord, yeve ich al,
> For everemo, myn hertes lust to rente.
> For nevere yet thi grace no wight sente
> So blisful cause as me, my lif to lede
> In alle joie and seurte, out of drede.
>
> (827–33)

Love is celebrated as a cause of "joy" and "surety," a compound of the highest moral virtues capable of assimilation into the order of courtliness:

> This is the righte lif that I am inne,
> To flemen alle manere vice and synne.
>
> (851–52)

Only those who have felt its influence can speak truly of its transforming potency. They—and they alone—are privileged to know that to love is to be raised above the common human order, replacing "dread" by the serene assurance of fulfillment:

> But I with al myn herte and al my myght,
> As I have seyd, wol love unto my laste,
> My deere herte, and al myn owen knyght,
> In which myn herte growen is so faste,
> And his in me, that it shal evere laste.
> Al dredde I first to love hym to bigynne,
> Now woot I wel, ther is no peril inne.
>
> (869–75)

Once again, reaction to this poignant evocation of beauty will not be simple or onesided. Antigone's song has expressed the eternally attractive romantic fantasy, the notion that love implies no peril, that its devotion is, quite simply, "for ever." By the end of Criseyde's story we shall know that what may be true of the love called "charity" is not, however human it may be so to desire, capable of being sustained on the level of romantic passion.

Criseyde, indeed, senses the truth of this. When her sister's "clear" tones have died into silence, her reaction hovers between conviction and doubt. Told that the maker of the song lived in "honor" and "joy," she comments wistfully: "Forsothe, so it semeth by hire song" (883), but she goes on to sigh and to ask whether such "bliss" exists between "Thise loveres, as they konne faire endite?" (886). The use of the word *endite* points clearly to the literary, and therefore limited nature of these transports. "Ye, wis" says "fresshe Antigone the white" in reassurance; but she adds that "the parfite blisse of love" (891) is, of its nature, separated from physical satisfaction: a point humanly open to question and in any case not suggestive of the kind of love that Pandarus is busily promoting and that Criseyde will soon enjoy with Troilus. "Can such love exist?" we are left asking, or is it a beautiful fantasy, capable of touching expression in the "enditing" of poets, but inaccessible to the ordinary range of mortals who "wenen all be love, if oon be hoot" (892) and involving a typically equivocal parallel with the happiness enjoyed by "saints" in heaven:

> Men mosten axe at seyntes if it is
> Aught fair in hevene (why? for they kan telle),
> And axen fendes is it foul in helle.
>
> (894–96)

Antigone's song has celebrated one aspect of love, idealizing and ennobling, and has carried us with it for as long as the echo of the music sounds in minds that their very humanity disposes to receive it. We are not to think that Chaucer intends us to be dismissive of what the song so movingly affirms; but another reality, which is balanced against it throughout the course of the poem, is implied in the wistful quality of Criseyde's reaction and confirmed in the erotic implications of her feverish dreams of the nightingale's song—song of violent passion, rape, and death—and of the eagle tearing out her heart (918–31).

After this interlude the moving force of the story passes decisively into the hands of Pandarus, as he moves "busily" between the lovers, drawing together the threads of his intrigue. The benevolent, sentimentally inclined uncle tends increasingly to be replaced by the tempter, the conscious and artful contriver of "situations." As he maneuvers first to bring Criseyde to Troilus on his sickbed in his brother's house and then to the decisive meeting at his own dwelling, a view of time as something to be seized, forced into conformity with the compulsions of natural desire becomes to an increasing degree characteristic of his benevolent "philosophizing." The insufficiency that his plausible claim to realistic common sense cannot finally cover will emerge later, exposed by the onward movement of events to their desolate conclusion. It will appear then as a fundamental truth governing our final understanding of this "tragedy" that men and women are required, as a natural condition of their being, to accept and live within the rhythm that their time imposes rather than to seek, unilaterally and impossibly, to bend its course to the ends that their wills propose as desirable.

2

The third book, central to the balanced structure of the poem, can be seen both as a consummation and the beginning of a fall. By bringing his three principal characters into interlocking relationship within the flow of a tensely onward moving action, Chaucer achieves effects of narrative perspective and sympathetic human concern that are without precedent in English, and perhaps in European literature. In the transports of a few intensely experienced hours, Troilus rises briefly to enjoyment of the "heaven" that is offered to those who follow the compulsions of desire under the auspices of changing Fortune. In obtaining this end he places himself in the position of Fortune's "fool" and surrenders his privilege of responsible freedom. His "bliss," intense and real while it lasts, requires the darkness of night for its enjoyment and is shadowed by the thought of returning day.

The dedication in the proem is, appropriately, to Venus, "Joves daughter deere." The emphasis is on the "bliss," the "plesaunce," that love offers to the "gentil hertes" of its initiates, who are disposed to find in it a source of "hele" and "gladnesse." The power of love is celebrated as a divine attribute that gives value—"worth"—to all created things, which in the absence of its sustaining force may not "endure":

> In hevene and helle, in erthe and salte see
> Is felt thi myght, if that I wel descerne;
> As man, brid, best, fissh, herbe, and grene tree
> Thee fele in tymes with vapour eterne.
> God loveth, and to love wol nought werne;
> And in this world no lyves creature
> Withouten love is worth, or may endure.
>
> (3. 8–14)

The voice that speaks here, although it makes use of "Boethian" language, is close to the poet's own: the voice of the Chaucer who will open *The Canterbury Tales* with a celebration of the annual renewal of life and who is concerned, in relation to the story he is now unfolding, to give "love"—even in the form of the service of Venus—its due as a natural manifestation of life. Once again the language combines terms proper to the "love" code with explicit Christian echoes. "God," we are reminded, "loveth," and the creation is bound together in bonds of love. Under this high patronage love is celebrated in terms of "light," the age's central symbol of spirituality and reason, and the "plesaunce" it offers is presented as "goodly, debonaire," a force that, in a direct echo of Francesca's famous phrase in the *Inferno*, is "ay redy to repaire . . . to gentil hertes."[12] The courtly language, and the necessary limitation of the poem's hero to the pagan terms available to him, act no doubt as a limiting factor upon what is here so eloquently affirmed. There are other attitudes to "desire," which the course of the story will reveal, but this need not lead us to attempt to turn the poet into a didactic moralist concerned to impose upon his matter the harsh judgment that a less balanced temperament might derive from the most respectable "authority."[13]

The decisive meeting between the lovers, which is explored at length in this central book, serves as a comment on this lofty preface. Criseyde has been induced to spend a convivial evening at her uncle's house and Troilus, having taken care to cover his tracks by letting it be known that he has gone to the temple of Apollo to consult the oracle on matters to do with the siege, holds himself in readiness to join her there. After an evening passed in laughter and courteous dalliance, as Criseyde prepares to take her leave, Fortune—"executrice of wyrdes" (617)—intervenes. The use of the Old English word is significant. The *wyrdes* are the Fates, which work out their obscure designs for men and women through the influence of the "stars." These present themselves in threatening conjunction and a "smoky reyn" (628) prevents her from leaving the house. To Pandarus this development, which he cannot have foreseen but which his ever-present resourcefulness is ready to turn to good use, comes as a godsend. "Now were it tyme a lady to gon henne!" (630), he comments gleefully, and Criseyde—fearful as ever—accepts the inevitable with good grace. The feasting is resumed, the "void" of the wine drunk and the shutters drawn to produce a comfortably sheltered interior as all retire, and the rain continues to fall and the wind to blow outside.

By now thoroughly at home in his role as busy impresario of love, Pandarus coaxes Criseyde into bed with expressions of avuncular reassurance. Skilled in all the circumstances of the "olde daunce" (695), he lets in the expectant Troilus, stressing that the moment of "celestial" happiness is at hand:

> Make the redy right anon,
> For thow shalt into hevene blisse wende.
>
> (703–4)

Animated by the offered prospect of "heaven" and begging for "grace" from "blisful Venus" (705), spurred on by Pandarus's gibes at his "mouses herte" and by his reassuring jest "Artow agast so that she wol the bite?" (736–37), Troilus anxiously awaits the summons that will bring him to the consummation of his bliss.

In what follows the approach to the climax is superbly managed to the maximum of dramatic effect. The emphasis is on the trusting security of those at rest within—"Ful sikerly they slepten alle yfere" (746)—and, beyond this, on stealth, on the "soft" (749), silent closing of the door behind Pandarus as he enters the bedchamber to reassure the waking, fearful Criseyde and to enjoin her to the secrecy that her situation seems to impose:

> "What! which wey be ye comen, *benedicite?*"
> Quod she, "and how thus unwist of hem alle?"
> "Here at this secre trappe-dore," quod he.
> Quod tho Criseyde, "Lat me som wight calle!"
> "I! God forbede that it sholde falle,"
> Quod Pandarus, "that ye swich folye wroughte!
> They myghte demen thyng they nevere er thoughte."
>
> (757–63)

"It is nought good a slepyng hound to wake" (764): though it may be that "sleeping hounds" of more than one kind are on the point of being roused.

Pressed in the direction that finally corresponds to her desires, and perturbed by her uncle's invented report that Troilus is jealously suspicious of her suspected relationship with a certain "Horaste" (797–98), Criseyde reacts with apprehension. She offers to reassure her lover as to the "trouthe," the trust that he may rightfully place in her. She will do this, however, "to-morrow" (848). She also reflects at some length on the brittle inconstancy of

> worldly selynesse,
> Which clerkes callen fals felicitee:
>
> (813–14)

happiness that, as she ruefully recognizes, "Imedled is with many a bitternesse" (815). The argument, which once again follows Boethius closely[14] in the process of echoing some of the most persistent commonplaces of "clerkly" thought and moral exhortation, relates her predicament to the underlying "philosophy" that governs the development of the tragedy. "Mannes joie unstable" is, Criseyde reflects, a combination of two elements. It rests, on the one hand, on unawareness of its transitory nature, and in this case it is unreasonable to think of it as in any way valid; for, as she observes,

> how may (a man) seye,
> That he hath verray joie and selynesse,
> That is of ignoraunce ay in derknesse?
>
> (824–26)

If, on the other hand, the same man is truly aware that his happiness cannot endure, it would seem that the awareness must affect his prospect of present felicity; for, in this case,

> The drede of lesyng maketh hym that he
> May in no perfit selynesse be.
>
> (830–31)

The touch of gentle skepticism implied, for an attentive reader of Chaucer, in the phrase *clerkes callen* should not escape us here; but the ambiguity of *selynesse*—a word that he can use to convey either real happiness or a naive trust in the possibility of finding it—is close to the deeper senses of the poem. "Ther is no verray" (true) "weele in this world here" (836). It is not by accident that Criseyde unburdens herself of these forebodings as she approaches the climactic moment of her relationship with her lover; but they do not lead her to what the "philosophy" underlying the poem would seem to advance as the appropriate conclusion, one that would avoid the extremes both of moralizing rejection or of conferring an impossible finality upon the real joys of the present, but merely to tinge with rueful bitterness her foreseen surrender. Indeed, as Chaucer would no doubt have us recognize, it may be beyond human possibility to do more; but, in this event, men and women alike will finally have to accept the limitation of their happiness that the recognition implies.

The approach to the climax maintains to fine effect a drama of tensely developed exchanges. Troilus, having made his entrance under cover of secrecy, finds his mistress initially speechless with embarrassed surprise—

> She kouthe naught a word aright out brynge
> So sodeynly, for his sodeyn comynge—
>
> (958–59)

while Pandarus, his purpose achieved, retires tactfully to the fireplace, using the light it gives to occupy himself with "an olde romaunce" (980). As the moment of truth approaches, comedy—sustained to the limit as Troilus swoons in "the crampe of deth" (1071) and is cast into bed unceremoniously deprived of his shirt—merges into the poetry of passion. The comparison at this point of Criseyde to a songbird in the grasp of the bird of prey—

> What myghte or may the sely larke seye,
> Whan that the sperhauk hath it in his foot?—
>
> (1191–92)

introduces a remarkable, if temporary, reversal of roles as Troilus prepares to enjoy what the "gods" seem to offer him by way of "heaven." We sense the measure of his sensual recovery from his swooning, lovesick moods as he comes to feel that the prize he has so obsessively coveted is at last in his grasp:

> Now be ye kaught, now is ther but we tweyne!
> Now yeldeth yow, for other bote is non!—
>
> (1207–8)

a notable change of tone, indeed, though not one inconsistent in terms of character, from the romantic sentimentalist of the earlier part of the poem.

Criseyde responds to the inevitable (and, of course, to more than that) by making her answering surrender:

> Ne hadde I er now, my swete herte deere,
> Ben yold, ywis, I were now nought heere!
>
> (1210–11)

Once again, the narrator inserts his enthusiastic comment, playing on the contrast between "heling" and "siknesse," "bittre drynke" and "gladnesse" (1212–15) and urging Criseyde's fellow-women, as readers and audience, to accept this happiness as and when it offers itself:

> For love of God, take every womman heede
> To werken thus, if it comth to the neede.
>
> (1224–25)

Truth or illusion, irony or simple-minded enthusiasm? We are surely meant to ask, but not too readily to answer. Whichever it may be, Criseyde, responding to her lover's expression of dedicated "trouthe and clene intente" (1229), winds herself about his body "as aboute a tree, with many a twiste / Bytrent and writh the swote wodebynde" (1230–31): a "sweet" embrace indeed, but one that may end by choking the plant to which it clings. Criseyde has "opened her heart" generously to the lover who seems to offer relief from her insecurity:

> And as the newe abaysed nyghtyngale,
> That stynteth first whan she bygynneth to synge,
> Whan that she hereth any herde tale,
> Or in the hegges any wyght stirynge,
> And after siker doth hire vois out rynge,
> Right so Criseyde, whan hire drede stente,
> Opned hire herte, and tolde hym hire entente;
>
> (1233–39)

but even as the narrative responds to this surge of confidence, the comparison with the nightingale recalls the tragic tale of rape in the story of Procne to cast a shadow of foreboding upon the moment of achieved consummation. In Troilus, too, death and "sickness" are intertwined as he surrenders to "present gladnesse" (1244), carrying with him the narrator—but not, it may be, altogether the poet, who has the tragic conclusion firmly in mind as he approaches the long-awaited climax of his story.

The sensual beauty of Criseyde is celebrated, at this moment of achieved climax, in terms not the less moving for being the reflection of an ideal of physical perfection familiar in much contemporary literature and painting:

> Hire armes smale, hire streghte bak and softe,
> Hire sydes longe, flesshly, smothe, and white
> He gan to stroke, and good thrift bad ful ofte
> Hire snowisshe throte, hire brestes rounde and lite:
> Thus in this heven he gan hym to delite,
> And therwithal a thousand tyme hire kiste.
>
> (1247–52)[15]

We are not to fail to respond to what is positive, life-reflecting in this expression of sensual fulfillment; but we shall note that the effect of Troilus's sensual triumph is to make him lose all control or understanding of himself ("what to don, for joie unnethe he wiste") and to place, by the very limitation to sensual contact, the kind of "heaven" that such love achieves. It is a "heaven" that the poet's detached and understanding vision proposes as at once valid, insofar as it answers to a true compulsion of life, and precarious inasmuch as it substitutes a part for the whole, seeking the illusory shadow of permanence that as men and women we so persistently and naturally desire, in what must remain by its very nature a transitory exaltation.

Confirming this central ambivalence Troilus combines "Charite" and "Citherea the swete" (1254–55), bringing together in a significantly confused evocation the two faces of love that coexist through the poem. In pursuit of a love that echoes the opening invocation by being seen through the eyes of its devotees as "benign" and "holy bond of thynges" (1261), he kisses Criseyde, of whom we are told with a disarmingly candid return to comedy, that she "certein . . . felte no disese" (1276) at this. He goes on to speak in familiar courtly terms of his unworthiness and of his intention to come to "amendment" through the "high service" (1288) to which he stands committed. Criseyde is to be the "star" by which he will guide his life to live or die. She is to illuminate his "ignorance" so that he may not do her displeasure. All this is familiar ground. We are to understand that this dedication to love in "trouthe and diligence" (1297) is, for all its intensity of dedication, close to a kind of idolatry. This does not mean that we are to ignore the positive implications, always serious in Chaucer, of "trouthe," the trust or faithful commitment that renders any human relationships, and indeed life itself, meaningful. As always, the balance of truth and self-deception needs to be firmly and delicately maintained. Criseyde, as she receives these statements of dedication from her lover, certainly intends to remain "true" to him, answering his trust with her devotion; but the story will end in her betrayal of him.

She responds, indeed, to these high-flown statements in words that echo those appropriate to religious devotion:

> myn owen hertes list,
> My ground of ese, and al myn herte deere.
>
> (1303–4)

"Welcome, my knyght, my pees, my suffisaunce!" (1309). These are terms that orthodox thought, reflecting perhaps a proper sense of human realities, would find excessive as addressed to any mere human being. At this point the narrator, as though aware of the uneasiness that such language is likely to inspire in his readers, confesses himself unable to find words to match the "evidence" of his original, and is content to allow his telling of the story to stand under correction from those who—unlike himself—have "ben at the feste / Of swich gladnesse" (1312–13) and who may be said to have "felyng . . . in loves art" (1333).

After this parenthesis we return to the lovers who, as we have been told, passed the night together "betwixen drede and sikernesse" (1315). Even as they clung together they feared "That al this thyng but nyce dremes were" (1342). The downward pull of the narrative is beginning to assert itself against the transports of sensual fulfillment. Troilus, as he kisses Criseyde's "eyen two," addresses them as the cause of "woe" to himself, calls them with the suggestion of a trap "humble nettes of my lady deere" (1352–55). At the same time, as he stresses the reality of the "bond" that unites them his tense emotional state dissolves into renewed sensual surrender:

> Therewith he gan hire faste in armes take,
> And wel an hondred tymes gan he syke,
> Naught swiche sorwfull sikes as men make
> For wo, or elles when that folk ben sike,
> But esy sykes, swiche as ben to like,
> That shewed his affectioun withinne;
> Of swiche sikes koude he nought bilynne.
>
> (1359–65)

Once again it is left to the narrator to enter his very human protest against those who may be unwilling to take these passionate transports at their own estimate. The "niggardly," ungenerous enemies of love may choose to consider the behavior of its devotees as a madness or "folye"; but such carping critics will surely suffer the consequences that he is happy to wish for them: "God yeve them meschaunce, / And every lovere in his trouthe avaunce!" (1384–86).

All this, however, and a further celebration of the joys of night, cannot prevent the inexorable return of day. Criseyde, like so many poetic lovers before and after her, can only curse its arrival and desire that the darkness could be bound "faste . . . to oure hemysperie" and "nevere more" leave them (1439–40). The exclusion of light, bringing with it the rejection of reason, has been a necessary condition for the continuation of her happiness. Troilus too grieves at the thought of separation. "The blody teris from his herte melte" (1445), and as he clasps her again to his arms he joins her in denouncing the day for cutting short the joys that "nyght and love han *stole* and faste iwryen" (1451). Criseyde has become for him the "welle and roote" (1473) of his being, and upon her continued presence the very possibility of continuing life seems to depend: "Syn that with yow is al the lyf ich have" (1477). Enslavement to passion is implied in his confession that "desyr" so "biteth" him that he must be "ded anon, but I retourne" (1482–83). The effect is to raise in his mind premonitory intimations of doubt. If he could be certain of her continuing faith, he could feel blessed in the possession of a thing that "Me levere were than thise worldes tweyne" (1490). The "two worlds" have been interpreted to mean "the realms of both Greece and Troy," or— rather more vaguely—"two worlds such as this";[16] but it seems possible that there is at least a sense suggested of "this world and the next," which would carry on the religious parallel that runs so persistently through the poem. Criseyde, always less ready to trust the validity of her feelings, swears in reply to keep truth, setting her love in contrast to what she feels, even as she swears, to be a contrary reality in things. There is something not unlike desperation in her plea that faith be answered with faith:

> Beth to me trewe, or ellis were it routhe . . . .
> Thus seyde I nevere er this, ne shal to mo.
>
> (1511, 1514)

Clinging to the "truth," which they feel is beginning to slip from their grasp, the lovers anticipate more truly than they know the desolate outcome of their story.

As though in confirmation of these uneasy premonitions, Fate— *Fortuna maior*[17]—intervenes to impose separation. "It mot nedes be" (1520): after a last frenzied clinging together, Troilus takes his leave "with swich voys as though his herte bledde" (1524). The rest of the canticle, whilst maintaining the balance of contrary "truths" so finely struck, is marked by the downward trend that will from now on prevail in the development of the "tragedy." Wrung with the sweet, equivocal "peyne of sharp desir", Troilus wishes only to return to the "plesaunce" he has left behind him. He fails to find release in sleep,

> and verraylich, of thilke remembraunce,
> Desir al newe hym brende, and lust to brede
> Gan more than erst.
>
> (1545–47)

"Remembrance," the memory of past sweetness, is replacing present pleasure as the moving force of emotion between the lovers. Criseyde's thoughts are fixed equally, though in a less illusory way, on the reliving of the past. When Pandarus lets drop his knowing hints about the events of the night—

> "Al nyght," quod he, "hath reyn so do me wake,
> That som of us, I trow, hire hedes ake"—
>
> (1560–61)

she greets him in the light of her sense of a sad return to daylight reality as the "fox" she feels him to have been:

> And ner he com, and seyde, "How stant it now
> Thus mury morwe? Nece, how kan ye fare?"
> Criseyde answerde, "Never the bet for yow,
> Fox that ye ben! God yeve youre herte kare!
> God help me so, ye caused al this fare,
> Trowe I," quod she, "for al youre wordes white,
> O, whoso seeth yow, knoweth yow ful lite."
>
> (1562–68)

This is in part a discovery of the unwelcome truth, but also the reaction of one who senses that she has rashly committed her being and who is now anxious to place upon other shoulders the blame for what has been done. It is perhaps as near as we get to seeing Pandarus as the cynical go-between, the mature contriver concerned to derive vicarious pleasure from the contemplation of what he himself is unable to perform.

Criseyde, indeed, in her mood of the "morning after," is realist enough to see the reality of her situation. Beyond this realism, she knows also that her own instincts have led her to accept her uncle's devices; and so it is not long before awareness of this connivance leads her to forgive him. After covering her face with the sheets and blushing "for shame al reed" (1570), she allows him to take his familiar liberties with her, "prying" into the bed and imposing himself in his own way:

> With that his arm al sodeynly he thriste
> Under hire nekke, and at the laste hire kyste.
>
> (1574–75)

We are told that she "Foryaf, and with here uncle gan to pleye, / For other cause was ther noon than so" (1578–79): rather, perhaps, as though Eve should forgive the serpent who tempted her to the act that lost for her (and for Adam with her) the right to live in the Garden of Paradise.

Having accomplished this part of his mission Pandarus, expeditious as ever—"nought ones seyde he nay" (1587)—returns to Troilus, whom he finds predictably in bed. The young man, kneeling as to a celestial messenger, thanks his mentor for having "in hevene ybrought my soule at reste" (1599), saving him from the torments of "hell." In return for this equivocal "salvation" he is ready to "sell" his life "a thousand tymes" (1601–2) in grateful repayment.

Pandarus, though no doubt gratified by this reaction, is realist enough to respond in a more considered way. He compares Troilus's new happiness to the realization of desired beatitude, echoing the poem's persistent undertheme by coupling the attainment of celestial "felicity" with the satisfaction of the desires of the flesh:

> Pandare answerd, and seyde thus, that "he
> That ones may in hevene blisse be,
> He feleth other weyes, dar I leye,
> Than thilke tyme he first herde of it seye."
>
> (1656–59)

Beyond this, he warns his friend of possible dangers lying ahead. "As gret a craft is kepe wel as wynne" (1634); for, as every moralist knows, though this he does not say, "worldly joie . . . it brest all day so ofte" (1637). More poignantly, and echoing Dante's Francesca, he reminds his protégé that

> The worse kynde of infortune is this,
> A man to han ben in prosperitee,
> And it remembren, whan it passed is.
>
> (1626–28)[18]

It is a fact, which men need realistically to accept, that those who place their trust on the favors of Fortune rely on a power that will, by its very nature, take away what it has so tantalizingly given. Pandarus's warning, uttered in relation to the love devotion and with the intention of urging Troilus to work at keeping what he has won, has a wider reference to the final sense of his tragedy.

Troilus's own words, indeed, though they continue to grasp at a kind of feverish happiness, begin to confront the inescapable reality. When he speaks of the "biting" of desire, or remarks that he "hadde it nevere half so hote as now" (1650), it is clear that a realistic understanding of the force of physical desire, far from the tenuous idealizations of conventionally poetic passion, moves the presentation of his state. Throughout these "morning after" exchanges there is a sense of returning daylight bringing with it for the lovers a sense of "dethis wownde" (1697). The night has been the element needed to bring them together. Now, when they have barely achieved their moment of felicity, the return of light imposes their separation. If they are to be seen as enjoying real happiness—as indeed the poetry of their meeting has movingly confirmed: "Agon was every sorwe and every feere" (1685)—their bliss remains dependent on the working of a power that imposes upon all human fulfillment a measure of impermanence: "thus Fortune a tyme ledde in joie / Criseyde and ek this kynges sone of Troie" (1714–15).

While accepting the truth thus expressed in the form of a rhyming "sentence," we shall once again avoid any simple or onesided judgment. The poem requires its readers to combine acceptance with detachment, to respond to the sensual transports so movingly celebrated while recognizing the shifting nature of the temporal foundations that both validate and limit it. It is appropriate that the central book should close, once more echoing the proem, on an eloquent celebration of love as a source of virtue and true sociability, a power

> that knetteth lawe of compaignie,
> And couples doth in vertu for to dwelle;
>
> (1748–49)

for it is love that establishes the harmony of the natural world: "ay heried be his myghtes!" (1757). As Troilus affirms the effect of this power, in words that recall Antigone's wistful song in the previous canticle[19]— words like those uttered in a garden and to Pandarus, the tempter, in person—the power of love is reaffirmed as the "bridle" that keeps the constituent elements of the creation in their appointed places; and Troilus, under its influence, prays to "God, that auctor is of kynde" (1765), that its sway may be so extended as to govern "hertes alle" that "from his bond no wight the wey out wiste" (1768). Against this background of universal harmony, love is seen as inspiring the hero to increased knightly prowess (1716–29), and his virtue finds celebration in the poetic expression of a spiritually exalted feudalism.

3

In the real world, however, the affirmations of poetry are not enough. The falling curve of the narrative in the last two books follows Fortune's wheel on its downward turn, as Troilus descends from the equivocal "heaven" upon which he has set his being. Having placed the center of his universe, exclusively and impossibly, in the love of a woman, he turns in vain for support to the resourceful Pandarus, only to find that his mentor can no longer help him. He is left to evade his problem by clinging to illusion until—inevitably—illusion fails him. Such is the "moral" upon which this part of the story rests. It only remains to add, once again, that it is presented in terms of poetry, not as a moralizing lesson but as a story rich in pathos and in the sense of human aspiration and human limit.

The new stage in the "tragedy" begins with a return to the war of Troy, which has rarely been foremost in our minds since the opening stages of the poem, but which now returns to impose its relevance in determining the lovers' fortunes. Under the shadow of a Trojan defeat Criseyde's father is moved to stress the service his treachery has afforded to his Greek masters and the extent of what he has lost in Troy as a result. Now that his reading of the stars tells him that Troy is about to fall, he proposes the exchange of his daughter for the warrior Antenor. This is proposed, debated in council, and agreed upon. The news leaves Troilus with a twofold problem. He must protect Criseyde's reputation in the eyes of the world, which means that their love must remain secret, and he must find means to prevent her departure. Railing bitterly against the "combreworld" (279) of which he sees himself as the victim, he turns once more to Pandarus, only to find that his friend is unable to offer even the shadow of comfort. "So confus that he nyste what to seye" (356) and weeping for "tender" pity—for he has always been a sentimentalist at heart—Pandarus joins his protégé in blaming Fortune for her fickleness and recognizes belatedly that no trust is to be placed in her operations.

His attempts to comfort his friend alternate between expressions of cynicism—"This town is ful of ladys al aboute" (401): "If she be loste, we shal recover an other" (406)—and arguments, in accordance with his "philosophy," that since love is no more than a matter of "casuel plesaunce," "Som cas shal putte it out of remembraunce" (420). Subjection to "cas," to the operations of blind chance, is indeed the sign throughout of a determinism that implies the rejection of the gift of choice on the exercise of which a responsible human life rests.

Indignantly rejecting the cynical advice so insensitively offered to him—"Kanstow pleyen raket, to and fro, / Nettle in, dok out, now this now that, Pandare?" (460–61)—Troilus refuses to adopt the other course that presents itself to him, which would be to "take" Criseyde by force, in rejection of the council. The reasons he gives for the rejection reflect creditably upon his motives. He believes that, as a responsible leader in Troy, he cannot think of spurning the public decision by "ravishing" his love. He is also aware that the unhappy war in which all—Greeks and Trojans alike—are involved had its origins in the "ravishing" of women (547-48); and he feels bound by the aristocratic code of conduct to respect Criseyde's wishes in this matter. To reveal their love by his actions would be to "disclaundre" the good name of his mistress, and as her "knight" he says that he "moste hire honour levere han than me" (570). Thus torn between "desire," which prompts him to "distourben" her, and "reason," which condemns such a course as brutal and intemperate (572-74), he finds himself in the hopeless position of one who sees that his love "increases" even as his hope of finding fulfillment in it grows "lasse and lasse."

Divided in this way, Troilus turns for consolation to sententious philosophizing. The long passage of verified Boethius that conveys his reflections and that takes up more than a hundred lines (960-1078) has puzzled readers who have found it a pedantic interpolation of tiresome effect. Neither here nor elsewhere should we give less than full value to Chaucer's readiness to poke fun at academic verbiage and confused pedantry. It is important beyond this, however, to see that Troilus is drawing an incomplete, finally a self-serving conclusion from the "authority" to which he is making appeal. If, as orthodox thinking asserts, God "foresees" all events infallibly—assuming that "foresee" is the right word to apply to a Being who exists outside time and who holds *all* times simultaneously present in his understanding—there would seem to be no place left for meaningful freedom of choice:

> Wherfore I say, that from eterne if he
> Hath wist byforn oure thought ek as oure dede,
> We han no fre chois, as thise clerkes rede.
>
> (978-80)

The conclusion, desolate though it may be in what it implies for human capacity to make significant choices, has the advantage for Troilus of allowing him to present his situation to himself as that of a helpless victim of circumstances beyond his control. He speaks in this way because he feels the need to see himself in the grip of "necessity," so as to absolve himself from responsibility for the tragedy that is on the point of overtaking his love. It is to be noted that his meditation paraphrases the *false*, or at least the incomplete reasoning of the complaining speaker in the *De Consolatione*, whose misfortunes led him to question the operations of "destiny" beyond his understanding or his power of acceptance. Troilus makes no reference to the reply, offered by the Lady Philosophy, that puts forward the Boethian "solution" to the problem raised by arguing that it is man's part to rise above his "fate" by recognizing that "purveyaunce"—Providence—works in ways that may seem, and indeed often are, beyond his understanding: ways, however, that the eye of faith, completing what reason can tell him, is able to find consistent with the existence, beyond his own necessarily limited, because time-conditioned vision, of an all-embracing and finally beneficent purpose governing the apparent vicissitudes of temporal existence. Boethius's full argument is not, as Troilus for his own ends would have it, directed at undermining man's belief in his freedom of choice or providing him with material for self-pity, but rather at freeing choice itself from the kind of subjection to blind "Fortune" that the entire story of his worldly involvement implies. What Troilus takes to be a proof, in which he perversely seeks comfort, of a fundamental irresponsibility in the direction of things is to be read more properly as an invitation to responsible and meaningful choice.

What remains of the fourth book is concerned with the last fevered meetings between the lovers. Criseyde, who has already been presented as burning "bothe in love and drede" (678) and unable, "for fere" (672), to ask for confirmation of what has been decided in the council, proposes that they should take refuge from reality in the only place where the illusion of relief may be found—in bed:

> But hoo, for we han right ynough of this,
> And lat us rise, and streght to bedde go,
> And there lat us speken of oure wo.
>
> (1242-44)

Even there, however, as we are told, "Whan they were in hire bed, in armes folde, / Nought was it lik the nyghtes here-byforn" (1247–48). She further seeks to reassure Troilus by promising so to contrive matters as to arrange for her return from the Greek camp. Her plans to this end reflect her confused state of mind. After placing her faith in her father's love for her, she goes on to dismiss him as "old" and "ful of covetise" (1369) and proposes to work on his weakness by guile and flattery to allow her to return to Troy. Troilus, anxious though he is to grasp at these remnants of illusion, which are strong enough to allow for a renewal of the "amorous daunce" (1431), knows that there is no real chance that she will be able to persuade her father or that, even if peace should be restored and Troy escape destruction, he as a traitor will be able to return:

> For which that wey, for aught I kan espie,
> To trusten on, nys but a fantasie:
>
> (1469-70)

a "fantasy" that here, as frequently in Chaucer, corresponds to the desire of men and women to see things not as they are, but as they would have them be. Troilus is realist enough to be aware that it is more likely that

Criseyde's father will use his authority to oblige his daughter to marry a Greek and to abandon a love that, on any realistic view, can have no future. Criseyde's response to her lover's recognition of the bleak truth is an indignant reproof of him for his lack of trust: "I se wel that ye mystrusten me" (1606). Urging him to keep faith in her absence, she concludes with a pathetic plea for pity: "For Goddes love, so beth me naught unkynde!" (1652), a far cry indeed from the young widow who had once thought of herself as "her own woman" and who had asserted, with a rash show of confidence that her own nature undermined, that no husband should "say to her *check-mate.*"

The final stage of the tragedy in the fifth book brings on the scene a suitor for Criseyde as different as may be from the "romantic," idealizing, self-obsessed Troilus. "Hardy, testif, strong, and chivalrous" (5. 802), Diomed—well able though he is to speak the language of courtly "service" when it suits his ends—observes the Trojan reality around him with a shrewd and calculating eye,

> As he that koude more than the crede
> In swich a craft.
>
> (5. 89–90)

Having quickly grasped the reason for Troilus's refusal to greet him, he turns his attention to Criseyde, considering, as he does so, that "He is a fool that wole foryete hymselve" (98). Sensing her need for security he offers her his "service" as a "brother," argues that Greeks and Trojans are alike in honoring "one god of Love" (143), and declares himself "Youre owene aboven every creature" (154). Her initial refusal to respond to these advances does not deter him, for he is well able to bide his time, confident that she will eventually need to turn to him for support.

Events justify his confidence as we follow the process by which Criseyde comes to accept what she finds to be her reality:

> Upon that other syde ek was Criseyde,
> With wommen fewe, among the Grekis stronge.
>
> (687–88)

She soon recognizes that she will never have her father's permission to return to Troy; but she is also aware that if she does not keep her promise to her lover he will conclude that she has betrayed him. If she should try to escape and return to Troy she is afraid of being taken for a spy or of falling into the hands of a "wretch" who may misuse her. Pathetically defenseless, she stresses her inability to foresee the future—perhaps because she is unwilling to accept what, at heart, she knows it offers—and clings, but by now only in words, to her intention to return.

Given this state of mind, her surrender is inevitable. Diomed's aim is to catch her in his "net," brushing aside the obstacle represented by her Trojan past. He is happy to see himself as a "conqueror," scornfully triumphant over his rival; and there is a revealing cynicism implied in the conclusion that, come what may, he will "namore lesen but my speche" (798). Perceiving that Criseyde is "Tender-herted, slydynge of corage" (825), he presents himself to her dressed for the occasion, "fressh as braunche in May" (844). In the course of casual conversation over "spyces and the wyne," he raises the question of her marriage prospects—

> And whi hire fader tarieth so longe
> To wedden hire unto som worthy wight—
>
> (862–3)

and stresses the futility of loving a Trojan. Troy, he is at pains to point out, is doomed:

> The folk of Troie, as who seyth, alle and some
> In prisoun ben, as ye youreselven se;
> Nor thennes shal nat oon on-lyve come
> For al the gold atwixen sonne and se,
> Trusteth wel, and understondeth me,
> Ther shal nat oon to mercy gon on-lyve,
> Al were he lord of worldes twies fyve!
>
> (883–89)

Finally, with an assumed bashfulness, he offers himself as her "servant" in love, declaring that he considers himself as "gentil man as any wight in Troie" (931). Emboldened by her unwillingness to reject his advances, he proceeds to address her directly as "herte myn" (939) and offers to speak further of the "service" he is disposed to offer.

Criseyde, as ever, temporizes. Pleading to be left alone with her sorrow, she agrees to receive her new suitor on the following day, but stipulates that he should not return to a subject that must be painful to her. Beyond that, she expresses pathetically her continuing concern for Troy—"O Diomede," she pleads against his ruthless insistence,

> I love that ilke place
> Ther I was born; and Joves, for his grace,
> Delyvere it soone of al that doth it care!
>
> (956–58)

and rejects all present talk of love. "I am disposed bet . . . Unto my deth" (984–85), she states, but adds, with the implied intention of keeping all her options open,

> What I shal after don, I kan nat seye;
> But trewelich, *as yet*, me list nat pleye.
>
> (986–87)

The implications of that "as yet" for the end of her story are clear, even as they reflect her present uncertainty. At some future time, "whan ye wonnen han the town" (990), matters may come to seem otherwise to her; meanwhile, if she should feel pity—"routhe"—for any Greek it would surely be for Diomed. For the moment she refuses to commit herself:

> I say nat therfore that I wol yow love,
> N'y say nat nay; but in conclusioun,
> *I mene wel*, by God that sit above!
>
> (1002–4)

The last phrase, spoken no doubt with a sigh that is both pathetic and self-conscious, shows us Criseyde taking refuge, perhaps beyond her conscious intention in the present, in an evasion that already implies submission to what she is coming to see as her reality.

What follows is the logical conclusion to this implicit surrender. Diomed presses his attentions with growing confidence and eventually takes possession of a pledge of faith in the form of Criseyde's glove. Alone and afraid of herself, she inclines to accept her lot among the Greeks, until Diomed's increasingly frequent and intimate visits "refte hire of the grete of al hire peyne" (1036). In her surrender she is less indulgent to her weakness than the narrator, who finds himself driven to blame the story as given to him for the need to record these unhappy realities. She recognizes that she has betrayed her faith and foresees what her fame will be to the end of (literary) time. "Thoroughout the world my belle shal be ronge!" (1062); but, seeing no way out of her predicament, she clings to the belief that "To Diomede algate"—at least—"I wol be trewe" (1071).

Parallel to these developments, and as the sad tale of betrayal takes its course, we have been shown Troilus in his despair, cursing his "gods" and "every creature," turning in his bed "as doth he Ixion in helle" and crying "piteously" on his lost mistress. His rhetorically developed laments focus on the loss of her physical presence, to the memory of which he clings with an intensity that collapses readily into the absurd:

> Wher is myn owene lady, lief and deere?
> Wher is hire white brest? wher is it, where?
> Wher ben hire armes and hire eyen cleere,
> That yesternyght this tyme with me were?

> Now may I wepe allone many a teere,
> And graspe aboute I may, but in this place,
> Save a pilowe, I fynde naught t'enbrace.
>
> (218–24)

The tone of these laments is at once "poetic" and sentimental. The poetry is real, but conditioned and limited by the nature of a content that the rhetorical emphasis, as it strives to give it expression, contrives to place. The effect is to convey the emotional state of one who is unable to contemplate steadily the reality of his own illusion, perhaps because at heart he is unable either to believe in it or to live without it.

Illusion, indeed, has by now become the obsessive content of Troilus's thought. A visit to the house of "kyng Sarpedoun" (431), engineered by Pandarus in the hope of distracting his friend from dwelling on his unhappy state, fails to achieve the desired effect. Returning from it to linger on the threshold of Criseyde's empty house, he is moved to a rhetorically conceived lament for the departed life of the "empty and disconsolat dwelling," for the "lanterne" that formerly gave it light, and for the "guide" of his life that has been so cruelly taken from him:

> O paleis, whilom crowne of houses alle,
> Enlumyned with sonne of alle blisse!
> O ryng, fro which the ruby is out falle,
> O cause of wo, that cause hast ben of lisse!
> Yet, syn I may no bet, fayn wolde I kisse
> Thy colde dores, dorste I for this route;
> And farwel shryne, of which the seynt is oute!
>
> (547–53)

To be noted here, once again, is the mixture—not to call it confusion—of spiritual and erotic content: on the one hand, "shrine" and "saint," on the other, "kiss" and the ring from which the ruby has fallen out. The content of the imagined "shrine" is, in the last analysis, sensual gratification dressed up as something other than it is, in a concession to self-regarding and self-limited sentiment. The stress lies on a real but equivocal "bliss." Because it is real, its loss can truly affect the lover as a kind of death, but because it is equivocal it can offer him no lasting consolation. As Troilus evokes the circumstances of the vanished past, we are made aware of the complexity of presentation that invites us to sympathize to the full but never to carry sympathy (whatever the intention of the supposedly "translated" text or of the "translator") to the point of sentimental identification. It is significant that Troilus should see himself as one of whose tragedy a "book" might be written "like a storie" (585).

Perhaps it is in this way that he would wish to see his predicament in his unhappy love.

Seeing himself in the present as "defet" and "pale" (618) and feeling that the eyes of the world are disparagingly upon him, Troilus reacts to the imagined pity of others with premonitions of his approaching death:

> Another tyme ymaginen he wolde
> That every wight that wente by the weye
> Hadde of hym routhe, and that they seyen sholde,
> "I am right sory Troilus wol deye."
>
> (624–27)

Readers of Dante's *Vita Nuova* will recognize the kind of love "psychology" that inspires this passage, and the criticism of "romantic" excess that moves it. In both works, differing as they do in presentation and often in attitude, "romantic" passion is seen as bearing within itself the seeds of its own demise. Dedicated to the cultivation of illusion, and with death and darkness prevailing in his heart—"Toward my deth with wynd in steere I saille" (641)—Troilus is reduced to sleeplessness at night. By day, as he and Pandarus stand on the walls of the besieged city looking for signs of Criseyde's return—"byjaped," as the poem cruelly puts it, "and staring aboute naught" (1119–20)—he tries to deceive himself into the belief that he can see her on the road—

> Have here my trouthe, I se hire! yond she is!
> Heve up thyn eyen, man! maistow nat se!—
>
> (1158–59)

when, as Pandarus is ruefully obliged to point out, what he actually sees is nothing but a peasant's cart.

By now, indeed, the tragedy is moving inexorably to its final stages. Troilus addresses a last letter to his love, affirming that all "joie" and "ese" have deserted him and pleading for her return, which alone can save him. She replies evasively with a short letter from the Greek camp, presenting herself as "sick" and in "distress" (1594), promising to return but unable to say when this will be, and ending with an assurance of continuing friendship, pleading that she has no practice in letter-writing and that "Th'entente is al, and nat the lettres space" (1630). When Troilus, facing his rival on the field of battle, sees the token he gave her as a pledge of his "truth" on Diomed's armor, he is obliged to acknowledge that "His lady nas no lenger on to triste" (1666) and turns for the last time to Pandarus, only to find that his mentor has no comfort to offer: "Ryght feyn I wolde amende it, wiste I how" (1741). Such is the end of so much busy and resourceful contriving. On the level contemplated by Pandarus and shared by his unhappy protégé, the ability of men and women to control the fate they have fashioned for themselves by the nature of their choices is indeed limited: "I kan namore seye" (1743).

Fortune, indeed, continues on her course, indifferent, it seems, to the tragedy of her victims. "But forth hire cours Fortune ay gan to holde" (1745). Criseyde is irretrievably tied to her new lover and Troilus left to his sorrow:

> Swich is this world, whoso it kan byholde:
> In ech estat is litel hertes reste:
>
> (1748–49)

a world perhaps beyond the ability of the narrator—or of the author he has "translated"—to see it steadily, though not on that account beyond the measure of understanding that Troilus—but only after his death—is about to achieve. The narrator prays at this point, not without an element of sententiousness, for help "to take it for the beste" (1750). Preparing to wind up the matter that has led him to a conclusion so contrary to his desire for his characters, he appeals to "every lady bright of hewe" not to be angry with him for having presented Criseyde as "untrewe." Women, he says, have often been "bitraised" (1779–81) and his advice to them, offered with a touch of wry humor that surely reads like an echo of Chaucer's own voice addressing his audience, is "Beth war of men, and herkneth what I seye!" (1785).

This direct address to the readers of the poem marks the transition to a conclusion that begins when Troilus is declared dead at the hands of the "fierse Achille" (1806). It leads to the much discussed and controverted "epilogue," which takes us rather farther than we have so far been but is not on that account unexpected. Though in some respects, perhaps, failing in unity of tone and harmony with what has gone before, it surely is not (as some have felt) a mere pious afterthought, but true to the poet's intention as it has been consistently developed. Only now, when the illusion on which he has chosen to rest his life has been shattered by the force of events pressing on human frailty, can Troilus, beyond finding in battle the death he seeks, begin to see the truth. What this is, his own thoughts on free will have, in their very incompleteness, implied; and now—carrying this implication to a logical conclusion—he has been brought to see that the kind of love to which he has chosen to dedicate his life must, in the very nature of things, fail to give the fulfillment that, unilaterally and impossibly, he sought from it.

Nor is this all. In contriving the tragedy of his hero, the poet has also been led to consider the nature, and possibly the limitation, of his own creative effort. As he finally pulls together the threads of his "matter," he finds himself forced to step outside it, overcoming the dichotomy between emotionally involved narrator and detached poet, which has been one of his main devices for conveying the emotional content of his story. It is the poet-creator who, at the line "Go, litel bok, go, litel myn tragedye" (1786), has already begun to take over from the supposed translator and to present himself as an author of the order of such as Dante when he associates what he has written with the work of the great poets of past ages (1791–92). The assumption—the claim—is that he has achieved his object by writing a poem that has made it possible for him to think of himself, with whatever proper degree of humility, as having made his contribution to the tradition of high, noble matter that the names of these poets imply.

To do this he has overcome the obstacle that the virtual nonexistence of a language suitable for this kind of utterance implies, an achievement indicated in the reference, which immediately follows, to the shifting, confused nature of English and the danger that what he has written may be handed down to future generations of readers in an imperfect form:

> And for ther is so gret diversite
> In Englisshe and in writynge of oure tonge,
> So prey I God that non myswrite the,
> Ne the mysmetre for defaute of tonge.
> And red wherso thow be, or elles songe,
> That thow be understonde, God I bisecheǃ
>
> (1793–98)

Beneath the seemingly conventional warning to the scribes there are literary issues of permanent importance. The whole question of what constitutes literature and the language in which it should be written is here implicitly raised. In the first place Chaucer is conscious of his poem as being *read* as well as sung or recited—in other words as being given to posterity, and so to a public each member of which will interpret its meaning in the light of his own assumptions and beliefs, as well as to an audience imagined as immediately before him. In the second place the meaning conveyed in this way will be conditioned by the nature of the language that constitutes the poetic medium. In this connection, the poet compares the instability, as he feels it to be, of his own tongue to the fixed adequacy of Latin, and implies that he has done for English what Dante had done for the vernacular Italian by writing the *Commedia*—in other words, forged an instrument suitable for high expression, capable of being thought of in connection with the recognized classics of the past. And, finally, he has at least insinuated that he thinks of himself, for the future, as not repeating this particular tragic achievement—great as he must feel it to be—but as a writer whose genius may lie in a rather different direction:

> Ther God thi makere yet, er that he dye,
> So sende myght to make in som comedye!
>
> (1787–88)

Comedy, of course, not simply in the sense of a poem to make readers laugh—though it may well, and properly, do that—but in that in which Dante used the word for the title of his poem: a work to reflect the variety of human experience—the kind of confused, fluctuating, and constantly renewing matter glimpsed by the poet at the end of *The House of Fame*[20]—under the guise of possible reconciliation and harmony. In this reference to comedy it is not entirely fanciful to see the germ of what was later to become *The Canterbury Tales*.

Having established these important points, Chaucer turns to the winding up of his poem. This requires that the author should step at the last outside his creation—outside, indeed, the limits of what we think of as literature—to consider where it stands in relation to what he and his age agreed in regarding as truth. Through his use of the narrator device, and by presenting his work as the translation of a story the terms of which he has not been free to change, he has been able to induce his readers to share in the values by which the tale is moved, to make them feel for and with his characters, to sympathize with their fate and, by extension, with the conception of love that governed their choices and led to their tragedy. At the same time, by telling a *pagan* story for Christian listeners or readers, who are aware that the values that move the telling are partial, even in some respects false, he has contrived that a proper distance be maintained between the audience and the events and motives related. Now, as the tragedy is being wound up, the poet-creator takes over unambiguously from the translator, replacing him and stepping, as it were, outside his creation to point to its significance for what is no longer the order of fiction, but—as it had to be for a medieval mind—that of reality. The author recognizes that both he and his audience, who are aware of sharing access to the truth, are in a position to look at the story of Troilus and his love with a proper measure of detachment, and recognizes that they can see what the characters of the tale as presented by the mysterious "Lollius" were prevented by their pagan situation from seeing in its completeness.

Precluded though he is from seeing the entire truth by the fact of having lived before the Christian revelation, Toilus can show at the last such measure of insight as was available to a pagan hero living in a pre-Christian dispensation. And so, following the device introduced into medieval literature by the *Somnium Scipionis* and already used by Chaucer in *The Parliament of Fowls,* Troilus, after meeting his end at the hands of Archilles, is translated to the "holughnesse of the eighthe spere" (1809)[21] and enabled to compare what he sees from this point of vantage with the vanity he has left behind him:

> And down from hennes faste he gan ayyse
> This litel spot of erthe, that with the se
> Embraced is, and fully gan despise
> This wrecched world, and held al vanite
> To respect of the pleyn felicite
> That is in hevene above, and at the laste,
> Ther he was slayn, his lokyng down he caste.
>
> (1814–20)

What he sees induces in him a new and disillusioned clarity. The false values that have governed his life present themselves to him as matter for repudiation, for a bitter recognition of his own blindness and that of all men who rely on their unaided vision:

> And in hymself he lough right at the wo
> Of hem that wepten for his deth so faste;
> And dampned al oure werk that foloweth so
> The blynde lust, the which that may nat laste.
>
> (1821–24)

This amounts to a comment on the values that the narrator, as servant of Love and its servants, has more or less tacitly sought to advance for the greater part of the poem. To a certain extent he has induced us, as readers, to respond generously to the human values that govern this tragedy of frustrated love; but the time has now come to leave dreams and shadows behind, to replace the narrator involved in the story he has been translating by the poet, who is in a position to see beyond the vision vouchsafed to Troilus—after his necessary death, in the place "Ther as Mercurye sorted hym to dwelle" (1827)—in the light of the true order of Christian charity.

Troilus's vision is conveyed with a certain sense of bitterness, which the rhetorical build-up of the following stanza stresses:

> Swich fyn hath, lo, this Troilus for love! . . .
> Swich fyn hath false worldes brotelnesse!
>
> (1828, 1832)

This, in pagan terms, is the inevitable conclusion of the story, a conclusion anticipated, with whatever additions of humanizing pity, from the beginning; but it cannot be the last word of a Christian addressing his contemporaries, a poet for whom Love, properly understood, reflects the creative purposes embodied in the universal order, which it has brought into being. The final step toward true understanding must lie, according to this reading of the story, in a recognition of the truth. This requires us, as readers, to see things as they are and not as a finally deluded and self-centered (though sometimes ennobling) remanticism would have them be. Troilus's love, far from leading him to freedom and fulfillment, has led him to subjection to impersonal Fortune and so to inevitable disappointment. Now, after he has died, he sees that behind his devotion there has been—together, no doubt, with much that has been deeply and humanly appealing—an element of what he has been taught by its necessary failure to call "blind lust," and he is ready to cast up his eyes to the reality in the light of which alone human love can become, not feigned or self-deceiving, unwilling to contemplate its own nature and the limitation on which it is based, but realistically and fulfillingly true.

The full expression of this realization is left not to the pagan Troilus, who is only able to see the disillusionment that his vision has imposed, but to the Christian poet now addressing his audience:

> O yonge, fresshe folkes, he or she,
> In which that love up groweth with youre age,
> Repeyreth hom fro worldly vanyte,
> And of youre herte up casteth the visage
> To thilke God that after his ymage
> Yow made, and thynketh al nys but a faire
> This world, that passeth soone as floures faire.
>
> And loveth hym, the which that right for love
> Upon a crois, oure soules for to beye,
> First starf, and roos, and sit in hevene above;
> For he nyl falsen no wight, dar I seye,
> That wol his herte al holly on hym leye.
> And syn he best to love is, and most meke,
> What nedeth feynede loves for to seke?
>
> (1835–48)

This conclusion is not, as some have believed, a mere moralizing afterthought or conventionally orthodox addition. It belongs rather to the essence of a conception by which the poem has been consistently animated: a conception expressed in medieval terms that may no longer be ours, but not on that account less true to the realities of human life. This, though he may not be in a position to see it completely, is what is implied in Troilus's awakening from the illusion that has made it possible for him to look in vain to see Criseyde returning from the Greek camp, and his readiness to see her, falsely and impossibly, under the guise of a peasant's cart. The extent of the human craving for self-deception, and its connection with the processes of imaginative creation by which, as human beings, we shape what we call our "reality," has rarely been better or more understandingly presented than in this great poem.

The whole story has shown, at appropriate moments and in no uncertain or grudging terms, what is good, positive, and life-promoting in romantic devotion. Even Criseyde, though faithless, has been presented as the victim of her circumstance, understood in her human frailty, where a more limited though at times powerful medieval sensibility—that, for example, of the fifteenth-century Scottish poet, Robert Henryson, in his impressive poem on the same theme[22]—would see her as perverse, treacherous, and sinful. Seeking to find consolation, humanly enough, for her unhappy condition in what is shown by the course of events to be fiction, Criseyde ends (but still humanly not as a moralizing "example") in betrayal; while Troilus, finally awakening from the world of illusion (but only after he has paid the price of illusion, which is death) learns that the only escape from the disillusionment that is seen to lie at the heart of the kind of love to which he has devoted himself is to cast his eyes beyond the action of Fortune, beyond the passing show that the world offers (and that is, in its own right, beautifully and necessarily alive), to the eternal order of true love, which alone can finally maintain and justify it.

From this point of view the lines that follow the moving affirmation just quoted of the order of Christian love and that are apt to strike a modern reader as overly unsympathetic—

> Lo here, of payens corsed olde rites,
> Lo here, what alle hire goddes may availle—
> (1849–50)

are seen as having a logical *raison d'être*, necessary to the spirit of a poem that rises finally and, again given its own terms, appropriately to the concluding prayer. Having asserted his community with his most distinguished English contemporaries—"moral Gower" and "philosophical Strode" (1856–57): the adjectives tell us something about the spirit in which the poem was conceived—Chaucer passes on to his conclusion:

> And to that sothefast Christ, that starf on rode,
> With al myn herte of mercy evere I preye,
> And to the Lord right thus I speke and seye:
>
> Thow oon, and two, and thre, eterne on lyve,
> That regnest ay in thre, and two, and oon,

> Uncircumscript, and al maist circumscrive,
> Us from visible and invisible foon
> Defende, and to thy mercy, everichon,
> So make us, Jesus, for thi mercy digne,
> For love of mayde and moder thyn benigne. Amen.
>
> (1860–69)

Here, necesarily, the language of religious devotion is conventional, in its expression.[23] The convention, however, is one that encompasses true feeling by channeling it into accepted forms, and we should be unwise to deny its relevance to the poem that is now ending. In this way—and, ultimately, in this way alone—temporal love, far from being renounced, is seen to be reclaimed in its proper setting, and the basic human partiality, which is that of clinging to the part (even the positive and necessary part) at the expense of the whole, can be fruitfully redeemed.

6
Postscript

In the last paragraph of the preceding chapter I have argued that the "epilogue" to *Troilus and Criseyde* represents something more than a conventional moralizing conclusion. Chaucer is likely to have written it in the confident conviction that his poem represented a major achievement both as regards his own work and in relation to the tradition of poetry in the English vernacular. A poet writing in English has succeeded in completing a work that can stand comparison, in scale and artistic seriousness, with the great Latin writers of the past and, more immediately, with the challenge represented in Italian by Dante's *Commedia*.

The last example, more particularly, may have been in Chaucer's mind as he completed his poem. This is not to say, of course, that *Troilus and Criseyde* is in any sense an imitation of Dante's great work. A great writer does not repeat the example of even the greatest of his predecessors, and we have seen that Chaucer in his earlier work, and more particularly in *The House of Fame*, approached Dante's achievement in a spirit that balanced respect with more than a touch of good-humored skepticism. By placing his "little tragedy" in the Homeric setting of the Trojan war and by relating each stage in its development to a philosophy of fate reflected in the significant motions of the stars, Chaucer evidently intended to give his tale of unhappy love a context more serious than anything he had previously attempted; and he did so in a way that provokes comparison with Dante's poem. In the actual presentation of his human tragedy, however, the differences emerge at least as clearly as the similarities. The theme of judgment, appropriate in the Italian poem as an image governing the presentation of human life *sub specie aeternitatis*, is one that the English poet approached with very notable uneasiness. Where Dante declares the theme of his work to be "man, as he is liable to rewarding and punishing justice in the exercise of freedom of his will,"[1]

Chaucer repeatedly expresses himself as unwilling to usurp the privilege of God by claiming to pass what must be, in the nature of things, a limited human judgment on the actions and choices of his characters. Where the Italian, consistently with the nature of his fiction, concentrates on the irrevocable nature of choices consciously and deliberately made, Chaucer, impatient with the very concept of finality in its application to human affairs, is apt to present the fluctuating behavior of his characters in a comic light and with a more humane and understanding tolerance.

In the epilogue there seems to be an attempt to go farther, to incorporate into the story that has just been brought to a close a judgment that has not been consistently present in its development. The effect seems to be to impose something like a Dantesque conception on a very different kind of story; but, if this is so, we can be forgiven for not remaining entirely convinced. The poet who inveighs so forcibly against the "cursed olde rites" of the pagan gods, and who claims to have demonstrated their deceptive nature so emphatically ("Lo, here": "Lo, here . . .") is not the Chaucer whose development we have traced in the earlier work, or to whom the body of the poem has accustomed us. Indeed, the whole development of the epilogue—even granting that it gives the story an appropriate and even necessary ending—leaves us with the sense of something rather arbitrarily attached to the body of the poem. Without doubting the moral sincerity that evidently speaks in the moving admonition addressed to "yonge fresshe folkes," it is possible to find the epilogue as a whole artistically troubling. It may indeed be that Chaucer himself felt less than happy in its regard and foresaw the need for working along different lines in the future. The references to some future "comedy" already taking shape in the poet's imagination may be, in this respect, significant. It may indicate a recognition on his part that his genius pointed finally in a direction different from that of Dante; that, recognizing the greatness of his predecessor and even their adherence to a common Christian philosophy, he owed it to himself to proceed for the future on a different path. It is thought probable that *Troilus and Criseyde* may have been completed in or around 1383; within a short space of time—not more than a year or two—Chaucer is likely to have embarked on the first stages of what was to become the "human comedy," essentially open-ended and distrustful of the human capacity for final statements, of *The Canterbury Tales*.

Notes

Chapter 1. Language and Poetics in Chaucer's Early Poetry

1. For Dante's thoughts on the possibilities of his own tongue for the writing of poetry, see his unfinished prose treatise in Latin, *De Volgari Eloquentia*.

2. *Inferno*, 4. 42 and 88–90. Dante's list differs from Chaucer's in replacing Statius by Horace. Statius, however, plays an important part in the *Purgatorio*.

3. See *Troilus and Criseyde*, 2. 22–28.

4. *Inferno*, 1. 63.

5. See *The Legend of Good Women*, F. 329, G. 255.

6. The body of scholarly opinion inclines to the view that only the first of the three fragments of the translation that are generally printed in editions of Chaucer's work can plausibly be ascribed to him.

7. Cf., among many examples, the portrait of Covetousness ("Covetyse") in *Piers Plowman*, C Text, 7. 196–203.

8. *Canterbury Tales*, 3. 1–828.

9. Ibid., General Prologue, 1. 208–69.

10. Ibid., 6. 329–968.

11. The date of *The House of Fame* cannot be fixed with any certainty. Somewhere near 1380 may be a reasonable conjecture.

12. For two examples among many of the use of the word in the sense of illusion, or willed self-deception, see *Canterbury Tales*, 4. 1577, 1610.

13. Cf., i.e., *Canterbury Tales*, 1. 3369.

14. *Purgatorio*, 9. 19–33.

15. Cf., *Canterbury Tales*, 1. 3186.

16. Once again, we cannot give an exact date for *The Parliament of Fowls*. Scholarly opinion is inclined to place it in the early 1380s, though other possibilities have been proposed. A variety of political and personal allegories have been suggested, but none of these interpretations seems to rest on a very solid foundation. See the note in F. N. Robinson's ed., p. 791.

17. The phrase was used by Ezra Pound to describe the mechanical effect to be avoided in the rhythm of true poetry.

18. The familiar aphorism can be traced back to Hippocrates.

19. The Wife of Bath is said in the General Prologue to be expert in "the olde daunce." See *Canterbury Tales*, 1. 476.

Index

Achilles, 69, 80, 138, 148n.13
Adam, 128
Aeneas, 55, 56–58
Africanus, 80–82, 84
Alanus de Insulis, 90, 149n.18
Amphiorax, 28
Antenor, 130
Antigone, 116–17, 129
Apollo, 119
Auerbach, Erich, 150n.7

Bacchus, 87
Bath, Wife of, 16, 147n.19, 150n.5
Beatrice, 20, 51, 60, 65
Blanche, Duchess of Lancaster, 33
Boccaccio, Giovanni, 102
Boethius, 44, 64, 70, 77, 88, 110, 121, 132
Book of the Duchess (Chaucer), 13–14, 17, 33–53, 54, 67

Calkas, 104, 130, 132
Canterbury Tales, The (Chaucer), 25, 31, 76, 96, 146, 147n.12, 148n.9
Ceres, 87
Charity *(Caritas)*, 77, 103
Chaucer, Geoffrey, 11–14, 16–17, 20–24, 25–31, 55, 62, 70–71, 79, 93–94, 103–4, 107, 109, 113, 118, 122, 124, 132, 138, 139, 140, 143, 145–46
Christ, 36, 53, 58
Cicero, 80
Clerk's Tale, The 149n.6
Commedia (Dante), 12, 56, 139–40, 145–46
Cornford, F. N., 149n.15

Criseyde, 25–32, 112, 114, 115, 116–17, 121–22, 123, 126, 133, 134–35, 137, 138
Cupid, 55, 82, 85, 100
Curry, W. C., 148n.2
Cytherea (Venus), 82, 124

Dante, 11, 20, 21, 25, 51, 56, 59, 60, 62–63, 64–65, 70, 139, 145–46, 147n.1, 148n.6, 150n.7
De Consolatione Philosophiae (Boethius), 44, 131, 148n.14, 150n.18
De Planctu Naturae (de Insulis), 149n.18
De Volgari Eloquentia (Dante), 12, 147n.1
Diana, 87
Dido, Queen of Carthage, 56–58, 67

Eagle (in *The House of Fame*), 17–20, 58–66
Eden, Garden of, 84–85, 108, 128
Edward II (king of England), 33
Eliot, T. S., 34, 148n.1
Eve, 128, 150n.15
Eyck, Jan van, 150n.15

Farinata, 150n.7
Filostrato (Boccaccio), 102, 149n.1
Francesca, 56, 119, 128
Franklin's Tale, The, 148n.9
Froissart, 13

Ganymede, 59
Gaunt, John of, 33
General Prologue *(Canterbury Tales)*, 93
Gower, John, 143, 149n.20
Gunn, A. F. M., 149n.19

153

Chapter 2. The Book of the Duchess

1. T. S. Eliot, "Tradition and the Individual Talent," in *Selected Essays* (London, 1932), p. 14.
2. On the medieval understanding of various kinds of dream, see W. C. Curry, *Chaucer and the Medieval Sciences* (London, 1960), chap. 8.
3. On the "spiritual" significance of dreams in medieval literature, see T. S. Eliot's distinction between the "high" and the "low" dream in his essay on Dante in *Selected Essays*, p. 248.
4. I adopt this term, current in modern critical discussion, with reservations and without any intention of tying it too explicitly to Chaucer's practice.
5. Ovid, *Metamorphoses*, bk. 11.
6. See p. 16 above.
7. F. N. Robinson, in the notes to his edition, says that the reference is "probably" to "the Roman emperor Octavian, a favorite figure in the Charlemagne romances, who married Florence, daughter of Dagobert, King of France" (p. 775). Others have preferred to see a more historical reference to the Emperor Augustus, and some have even speculated on possible allegorical significances attached to the number eight.
8. For the Boethian view of Fortune, see *De Consolatione Philosophiae*, 2. prosa 1, 58–114.
9. For a direct affirmation of Chaucer's sense of the importance of *truth* in human life, cf. the statement of Arveragus in *The Franklin's Tale*: "Trouthe is the hyeste thyng that man may kepe" (5. 1479). I have discussed the sense of this phrase, and the connection between *truth*, the sense of *trust*, and the implications of *betroth* in my essay on *The Franklin's Tale* in *The Literary Imagination* (Newark, 1981), pp. 114–15.
10. *Vita Nuova*, chap. 10.

Chapter 3. The House of Fame

1. Cf. *The Knight's Tale*, 1. 1956.
2. *Inferno*, 5. 70–142.
3. On the Chaucerian sense of "trouthe" see no. 9 above.
4. The story of Dido's love for Aeneas and of her death after he had abandoned her to pursue his providential mission is given in Book 4 of the *Aeneid*.
5. *Purgatorio*, 9. 19–33.
6. Cf., for examples of Beatrice's reproof of Dante for his intellectual and moral inadequacy, *Paradiso*, 1. 88–90: 2. 61–63: 3. 25–28.
7. *Inferno*, 2. 32.
8. It may be noted that the last line of the exposition—"Take yt in ernest or in game"—anticipates later Chaucerian uses of this phrase, which relate to his understanding of the nature of his art. Compare *The Miller's Prologue*, 1. 3186 and *The Manciple's Prologue*, 9. 100.
9. See 2 Cor. 12:2, echoed by Dante in various places in relation to his own "journey."
10. *Inferno*, 2. 28.
11. "La concreata e perpetua sete" (*Paradiso*, 2. 19).
12. See, among other examples, *Paradiso*, 26. 4–15.
13. Cf. "the fierse Achille" (*Troilus and Criseyde*, 5. 1806).
14. See Boethius, *De Consolatione Philosophiae*, 2, prosa 1, 81–115.

Chapter 4. The Parliament of Fowls

1. *The Owl and the Nightingale* may be dated ca. 1200.
2. See pp. 25–32 above.

3. *The Dream of Scipio* originally formed part of bk. 6 of Cicero's *De Re Publica*.
4. *Paradiso*, 22. 132–38.
5. *Troilus and Criseyde*, 5. 1806. See p. 138 below.
6. The idea of the "comun profyt," or of an individual's service to what we may call the "commonwealth," as an essential aspect of his human fulfillment, is one that finds expression elsewhere in Chaucer's work. Cf. *The Clerk's Tale*, 4. 431.
7. Cf. *Hamlet*, 2. 2. 396.
8. *Inferno*, 3. 1–9.
9. It may be noted that these words represent some of the principal obstacles encountered by the Lover in his quest in *The Romaunt of the Rose*.
10. *Purgatorio*, 28. In making this comparison, I do not intend to suggest that Chaucer necessarily had the Dantesque passage in mind when he wrote.
11. The use of "will" to indicate sensual desire is common in English poetry up to the sixteenth century. Compare Shakespeare's Sonnet 135.
12. Cf. the description of the Temple dedicated to Venus in *The Knight's Tale*, 1. 1918–66.
13. For a similar reference to Priapus, the garden-dwelling god, see *The Merchant's Tale*, 4. 2034.
14. On this subject, and in relation to what follows, it is still useful to consult Arthur O. Lovejoy, *The Great Chain of Being* (Cambridge, Mass., 1953).
15. *Timaeus*, 29D. This, and the passages that follow, are quoted from F. N. Cornford, *Plato's Cosmology* (London, 1937), p. 33.
16. *Timaeus*, 30C (p. 34).
17. *Timaeus*, 41C (p. 140).
18. Chaucer refers his account of Nature and the birds to the twelfth-century Latin author Alanus de Insulis in his *De Planctu Naturae*. He may also have had in mind similar passages in *The Romaunt of the Rose*.
19. For the meaning of *The Romaunt of the Rose* I have found it useful to consult A. F. M. Gunn's *Mirror of Love* (Lubbock, Tex., 1952). C. S. Lewis's *Allegory of Love* also contains valuable material.
20. The idea of a council of birds is familiar in medieval literature, both in English and in French. An example that Chaucer is likely to have known is found in Balade 35 by his contemporary John Gower, where the gathering is said to have taken place on St. Valentine's Day.
21. It has been argued with some plausibility that the poem is concerned with the attempts to arrange a marriage for the young Richard II to Marie, daughter of Charles V of France, in 1377–78. The interest of the poem seems to me, however, notably to transcend this possible occasion.
22. "Men shal nat maken ernest of game" (*The Canterbury Tales*, 1. 3186).
23. *The Canterbury Tales*, 1. 11.
24. Cf., in the first continuous fragment of *The Canterbury Tales*, the descent of the order of pilgrimage into disorder from *The Knight's Tale*, through the tales told by the Miller and the Reeve, to the abortive intervention of the Cook.
25. Cf., in *The Knight's Tale*, the unwillingness of Emelye to contemplate the pains and discomforts of the marriage yoke (*Canterbury Tales*, 1. 2304–6).

Chapter 5. *Troilus and Criseyde*

1. See C. S. Lewis, *What Chaucer Really Did to "Il Filostrato"*, Essays and Studies 17 (1932): 56–75.
2. At two points in the poem (1.394 and 5.1653) Chaucer states that he is following a certain "Lollius" who is also mentioned, together with a number of known writers of the past, in *The House of Fame*, 1468. On the difficulty of identifying "Lollius," and of relating him to any possible "source" for Chaucer's poem, see F. N. Robinson's note on p. 812 of his edition.
3. See *Troilus and Criseyde*, 1. 85–91.

4. It is possible that this, like other "Boethian" passages in the poem, were introduced into it by Chaucer at a relatively late stage and in the process of revision. On the subject of authorial revision in *Troilus and Criseyde* see R. K. Root, *The Textual Tradition of Chaucer's Troilus* (Chaucer Society, 1916) and the same author's edition (Princeton, N.J., 1926).

5. For an expression of this argument cf. Dante, *Inferno*, 7. 77–84 and the discourse on "gentillesse" in *The Wife of Bath's Tale*, 3. 1146–64.

6. Cf., in Shakespeare's version of the same story, Troilus' self-conscious references to his "wallowing" in "the lily-beds / Proposed for the deserver" (*Troilus and Cressida*, 3.2.11–12).

7. For a similar development in the work of Dante, with its implications for European literature as a whole, see Erich Auerbach's study of Canto 10 of the *Inferno* (the episode of Farinata and Cavalcanti) in *Mimesis* (Princeton, N.J., 1953), chap. 8, pp. 174–206.

8. See pp. 25–32 above.

9. For Priapus as the "god" of gardens and husbandry, see *The Merchant's Tale*, 4. 2034.

10. "I hoppe alwey behinde" (2. 1107) is Pandarus's own way of describing his unsuccessful pursuit of love.

11. See *Troilus and Criseyde*, 3. 253–63.

12. *Inferno*, 5. 100.

13. D. W. Robertson, Jr., in his *Study of "Troilus and Criseyde"* (*English Literary History* 19 [1952]: 1–37) seems to fall into excess in this regard in the process of saying much that is revealing and important for an understanding of the poem.

14. See *De Consolatione Philosophiae*, 2. prosa 4, 150–63.

15. One is reminded of representations of Eve in the Garden by such artists as Van Eyck and Roger van der Weyden.

16. See F. N. Robinson's note on p. 827 of his edition.

17. This is the "Fortune, executrice of wyrdes" of 3. 617 above.

18. *Inferno*, 5. 121–23. The phrase seems to derive from Boethius, *De Consolatione Philosophiae*, 2. prosa 4, 7–9.

19. See p. 116 above.

20. See p. 76 above.

21. The "eight sphere" is interpreted by most scholars as that corresponding to Mercury; in other words, the "eighth" in the Ptolemaic system counting downward from the Primum Mobile. See, on this question, John M. Steadman's *Disembodied Laughter: Troilus and the Apotheosis Tradition* (Berkeley, Calif., 1972).

22. Robert Henryson, *The Testament of Cresseid*, to be dated around 1500.

23. Chaucer is remembering here Dante, *Paradiso* 14. n. 28–30.

Chapter 6. Postscript

1. *Letter to Can Grande*, para. 8. The ascription to Dante of this famous Latin epistle has been questioned, but it seems that the balance of scholarly opinion is inclined to accept it as genuine. In any case, the question of authorship is immaterial in relation to the present argument.

Bibliography

Text

Chaucer, Geoffrey. *Works*. Edited by F. N. Robinson. 2d ed. Boston: Houghton Mifflin, 1957.

Critical Studies

Bennett, J. A. W. *Chaucer's Book of Fame*. Oxford: Clarendon, 1968.
———. *The Parliament of Fowls*. Oxford: Clarendon, 1957.
Bishop, Ian. *Chaucer's "Troilus and Criseyde": A Critical Study*. Bristol: Bristol University Press, 1981.
Clemen, Wolfgang. *Chaucer's Early Poetry*. London: Methuen, 1963.
Coghill, Nevill. *The Poet Chaucer*. London: Oxford University Press, 1967.
Curry, Walter Clyde. *Chaucer and the Medieval Sciences*. New York: Barnes and Noble, 1960.
Delaney, Sheila. *Chaucer's House of Fame: The Poetics of Sceptical Fideism*. Chicago: University of Chicago Press, 1972.
Dempster, Germaine. *Dramatic Irony in Chaucer*. New York: Humanities Press, 1959.
Donaldson, E. Talbot. *Speaking of Chaucer*. London: Athlone, 1970.
Gordon, Ida L. *The Double Sorrow of Troilus*. London: Oxford University Press, 1970.
Gunn, Alan M. F. *The Mirror of Love: A Reinterpretation of the "Romaunce of the Rose."* Lubbock, Tex.: Christian University Press, 1952.
Huppé, Bernard, and D. W. Robertson, Jr. *Fruyt and Chaf: Studies in Chaucer's Allegories*. Princeton: Princeton University Press, 1963.
Kean, Patricia. *The Art of Narrative*. London: Routledge, 1972.
———. *Chaucer's Love Vision and Debate*. London: Routledge, 1972.

Kirby, Thomas A. *Chaucer's Troilus: A Study in Courtly Love.* Gloucester, Mass.: Peter Smith, 1959.

Lawlor, John. *Chaucer.* New York: Harper, 1969.

Lewis, C. S. *The Allegory of Love.* Oxford: Clarendon, 1936.

———. *The Discarded Image.* London: Cambridge University Press, 1964.

Lovejoy, Arthur O. *The Great Chain of Being.* Cambridge, Mass.: Harvard University Press, 1953.

Muscatine, Charles. *Chaucer and the French Tradition: A Study in Style and Meaning.* Berkeley: University of California Press, 1957.

Payne, Robert O. *The Key of Remembrance: A Study in Chaucer's Poetics.* New Haven: Yale University Press, 1963.

Robertson, D. W., Jr. *A Preface to Chaucer: Studies in Medieval Perspectives.* Princeton: Princeton University Press, 1962.

Robinson, Ian. *Chaucer's Prosody: A Study of the Middle English Verse Traditions.* London: Cambridge University Press, 1971.

Seznac, Jean. *The Survival of the Pagan Gods.* New York: Oxford University Press, 1953.

Spearing, A. C. *Medieval Dream Poetry.* London: Cambridge University Press, 1976.

Speirs, John. *Chaucer the Maker.* London: Faber and Faber, 1962.

Steadman, John M. *Disembodied Laughter: Troilus and the Apotheosis Tradition.* Berkeley: University of California Press, 1972.

Collections of Individual Studies

Brewer, Derek S. *Chaucer and Chaucerians: Critical Studies in Middle English Literature.* London: Nelson, 1966.

Ford, Boris, ed. *The New Pelican Guide to English Literature: Vol. 1: Medieval Literature.* Harmondsworth: Penguin Books, 1982.

Shoeck, Richard J., and Jerome Taylor, eds. *Chaucer Criticism: Troilus and Criseyde and the Minor Poems.* Notre Dame, Ind.: Notre Dame University Press, 1961.

Wagenknecht, E., ed. *Chaucer: Modern Essays in Criticism.* New York: Oxford University Press, 1959.

Hamlet (Shakespeare), 149 n. 7
Henryson, Robert, 143, 150 n. 22
Hippocrates, 147 n. 18
Homer, 11, 69
Horace, 147 n. 2
House of Fame, The (Chaucer), 17–21, 25, 54–77, 101, 145, 147 n. 11, 149 n. 2

Iliad (Homer), 102
Inferno (Dante), 11, 56, 83, 119, 147 n. 2, 148 n. 2, 149 n. 8, 150 n. 5
Ixion, 135

Jugement du Roy de Behaigne (Machaut), 13
Juno, 16
Jupiter, 60

Knight's Tale, The, 148 n. 1, 149 n. 25

Legend of Good Women, The (Chaucer), 147 n. 5
Leonard, Saint, 55
Lewis, C. S., 149 n. 1
Lollius, 140, 149 n. 2
Lorris, Guillaume de, 16, 90–92
Lovejoy, Arthur O., 149 n. 14
Lucan, 11

Machaut, Guillaume, 13, 35–36
Macrobius, 80, 82, 88
Manciple's Prologue, The, 148 n. 8
Mercury, 141, 150 n. 21
Metamorphoses (Ovid), 37, 148 n. 5
Meun, Jean de, 16, 90, 92
Miller's Prologue, The, 148 n. 8
Morpheus, 16, 37, 38

Octavian, 40
Ovid, 11, 23, 37, 39, 148 n. 5
Owl and the Nightingale, The, 78, 148 n. 1

Pandarus, 25–32, 107–8, 108–9, 109–11, 111–12, 119–21, 127, 128, 130, 137–38
Paradiso (Dante), 60, 64–65, 80, 148 nn. 11 and 12, 149 n. 4, 150 n. 23

Parliament of Fowls, The (Chaucer), 21–25, 31, 78–101, 141
Paul, Saint, 64
Petrarch, Francesco, 70
Piers Plowman (Langland), 15, 22, 147 n. 7
Plato, 88–89, 149 n. 15
Pound, Ezra, 147 n. 17
Priapus, 86, 114, 149 n. 13, 150 n. 9
Procne, 123
Purgatorio (Dante), 20, 59, 85, 147 n. 2, 149 n. 10

Richard II (king of England), 149 n. 21
Robertson, D. W., Jr., 150 n. 13
Robinson, F. N., 147 n. 16, 148 n. 7, 149 n. 2, 150 n. 16
Romaunt de la Rose, The (de Lorris and de Meun), 13, 14–16, 36, 39, 90–92, 108–9, 149 n. 9
Root, R. K., 150 n. 4

Sarpedon, 136
Scipio, 80–82, 141, 149 n. 3
Seyx and Alcyone, 37–38, 41–42, 53, 67
Shakespeare, William, 22
Sonnets (Shakespeare), 149 n. 11
Statius, 11, 69, 147 n. 2
Steadman, J. M., 150 n. 21

Thebes, 28
Timaeus (Plato), 88–89
Troilus, 104–6, 107, 109, 112, 115, 120, 122–24, 124–25, 126–29, 130, 131–32, 135–37, 138, 140–42
Troilus and Cressida (Shakespeare), 150 n. 6
Troilus and Criseyde (Chaucer), 11, 25, 26–31, 102–44, 145, 147 n. 3, 148 n. 13, 149 n. 3, 150 n. 6

Valentine, Saint, 87, 92, 149 n. 20
Venus, 55, 58, 60, 82, 86–88, 89–90, 92, 100, 119
Vergil, 11, 12, 55, 57, 59, 148 n. 4
Vita Nuova (Dante), 47, 51, 148 n. 10
Vulcan, 55

Weyden, Roger van der, 150 n. 15

OHIO UNIVERSITY LIBRARY

Please return this book as soon as you have finished with it. In order to avoid a fine it must be returned the latest date mped below.